9789023634843

D1811097

CLWYD
LIMESTONE

CLYWD LIMESTONE

by
Stuart Cathcart

Photos by
D.Barker
and
S.M.Cathcart

CICERONE PRESS

Front Cover:
Kinberg, Pinfold North Buttress
Climber, Paul Stott

Back Cover:
Manikins of Horror, Craig Arthur
Climber, Malcolm Cameron

◁ *Sunday Driver, Twilight Tower Buttress*
Climber, Stuart Cathcart

© Stuart Cathcart 1983
First Published 1983

SBN 902 363 48 4

Published by Cicerone Press
Harmony Hall, Milnthorpe, Cumbria.

IF YOU LIKE ADVENTUROUS ACTIVITIES IN HILL COUNTRY YOU WILL ENJOY READING

CLIMBER & rambler

HILL WALKING/SCRAMBLING/ROCK CLIMBING MOUNTAINEERING/IN BRITAIN AND ABROAD

Available from newsagents, outdoor equipment shops, or by subscription (6-12 months) from Holmes McDougall Ltd. Ravenseft House, 302-304 St. Vincent's Street, Glasgow G2 5RG

CONTENTS

ACKNOWLEDGEMENTS

The compilation of this guidebook has by no means been a whirlwind affair. But from the birth of the idea of a guidebook to the area in 1975 to its completion in 1981, there have not been as many climbers involved in the work as the number of years in mention.

Numerous individuals said they knew someone, who knew someone, who made the first ascent of this or that. When it actually came to the crunch of producing an address or telephone number, so that I could answer the many questions I had or even just to talk to someone who I thought really knew some true facts about the area, virtually no one was forthcoming.

My acknowledgements are therefore limited to those friends who remained extremely patient, especially during 1980/81 when 99% of my own climbing was centred around the Eglwyseg Valley and they were willing to forfeit days in North Wales, etc. for days producing fine new routes locally. Many thanks therefore go to Gerald Swindley, Paul Stott, Mal Cameron, Tom Curtis, John Dee, Frank Bennett and Mike Hughes.

One or two people kindly wrote to me with helpful hints, but few with any real facts. Robin Tilston helped me by lending me one of the few copies of Bob Dearman's small guide to Craig y Forwen.

Of the principal contributors who I am greatly indebted to for making this mammoth task just that little bit easier are Paul Stott, for documenting and climbing all the routes on the Twilight Tower Buttress, which by the completion of his work he like myself had grown to love the quality and unique remoteness of the climbing in the Egywyseg Valley. The superb crag drawings were produced by Dave Whitlow (Wee Dave), who I must also thank for his excellent attentive ropework whilst seconding me on several shaky leads on first ascents. Norma Nicol for her notes on the geology to the area and Mark Hutchinson from the BMC for the help with the one or two access problems.

Many climbers scoff at other climbers who dedicate guidebooks and books to their wives but unless you have actually been involved in such an undertaking it is impossible to appreciate how much an occasional interest can become an obsession. Those around you do not necessarily suffer but they are unintentionally ignored for long periods at a time. I therefore have no qualms in dedicating this guidebook to my non-climbing wife, Alison, and thanking her more than anyone else for her patience and understanding.

INTRODUCTION

It is inevitable that every piece of rock in the British Isles will unfortunately one day be documented in texts such as this. Publishers will be almost redundant, pioneers will be left with nothing to find and athletic training will be on the everyday agenda for most climbers; what a statement! But considering the speed at which new rock is being devoured even in 1983 it is amazing that this range of hills and especially the splendid Eglwyseg Valley has remained almost untouched and out of heresay for so long, and could well have remained so. I think its late development has been mainly due to its geographical position, being between Snowdonia and the large cities of the north-west, many climbers have in the past preferred to venture into Wales than sample the Derbyshire type atmosphere locally. Climbers also tend to need to be led by the hand and until they have something to work from they are a little apprehensive about sampling.

To me the area has been like a toy for the past seven years, played with and left until a final realisation of the potential and beauty that this region has to offer spurred me to concentrate totally on the fulfilment of an idea. I consider myself very lucky to have been able to polish this gem often alone and almost always without the competition of others to reap the benefits of enjoying endless new routes in near perfect surroundings. I also feel sad in some ways that this guide book will undoubtedly promote considerable interest in the area and the atmosphere in which I made many of the first ascents will never really be savoured by other climbers, in the knowledge that there is not another climber anywhere on the crag, even on a Bank Holiday!

Throughout its compilation and in the finished article I have attempted to give as much attention to the beginner and low grade climber as I have the hot shot top grade man, by giving as much detail 'as possible' in the lower grades and as much detail 'as necessary' in the high grades. I have tried to work on the basis that climbing is an adventure sport and as such for the lower grade climber it is an adventure to actually do a climb and therefore he needs all the information possible, but for the high grade rat it is unnecessary to pamper him with minor details as he or she should be more attuned to making the best of very little. In order to back up this theory I have introduced a slightly new grading system, which is explained fully in the Technical Notes section and I think is a worthwhile developement for this type of guide. Similarly I could have filled the guide with crag photographs and diagrams, but with the exception of Craig Arthur and Monk's Buttress it would only be

7

pampering the climber when only a good description is necessary leaving the rest to the climber's judgement. The use of stars to indicate the quality of routes may seem a little over-used compared with other guides, but I feel that many authors are too sparing and in turn the system does not always work to its best advantage in spreading out the load of eager climbers from just a few top notch routes.

Finally, I hope that this area will not only gain popularity from its excellent climbing but as another good, much needed, poor weather climbing area. Being in the lee of the main mountains of Snowdonia this area is often dry when others are very wet.

HISTORICAL

The first record of climbs in this area appeared in 'Mountain Craft' in 1963. H.J. Tinkler, then an undergraduate at Liverpool University, realised the climbing potential of the Eglwyseg Valley in the course of his geographical studies, and described about 40 routes in his article. Apparently, a few climbs bore evidence of previous ascents, but most were first led by John Hesketh, notably Intensity, which remained the hardest free climb in the valley for almost a decade.

The majority of these routes were on Craig y Forwen, still the most popular of the Eglwyseg Crags, and on Twilight Tower Buttress. Craig Arthur, although mentioned as having been climbed, was only considered as being of interest to the artificial climber, for whom it was said to hold 'tremendous possibilities in airy situations'. John Clements, Martin Jones and Nick Hall were amongst the first to climb there in the early sixties, but their explorations remain something of a mystery which is unfortunate, as Clements in particular was one of the most forceful new route pioneers of his time. They were soon followed by Tom Hurley, Brian Riley and Dave Blythe, who pegged Nemesis, Scouser's Slab and Chota Peg (now The Big Plop) around 1964.

As elsewhere on limestone in the sixties, the Clwyd crags were regarded as good practice grounds for artificial climbing. Apart from Craig Arthur, evidence of such ascents could be found at Maeshafn Devil's Gorge; Craig y Forwen and Trevor Rocks around this time, although records were not kept. Many of these lines have become good free routes, such as Mathematical Workout, Hornbeam and Any Which Way.

Craig Arthur was given the stage for the next wave of significant development when in 1969 Bob Dearman and Dave Riley began to investigate the crag. Tom Hurley joined the team and together they produced the magnificent Girdle Traverse. Described at the time as *V.S.* with several aid pegs, it has since been free climbed at E2 and must rate as one of the highlights of the area. Dearman, with Martin Pedler, later added the fine free or mainly free routes of Swlabr, Badge and Scrapyard Thing, titles lifted from the albums by Cream, the original heavy rock supergroup, and indicative of Dearman's musical taste at the time.

Dearman described his routes in an article in 'Rocksport' in 1979 and appealed for information with a view to producing a guidebook to the Eglwyseg Valley. Unfortunately, this project never reached publication, and he eventually turned the information he had gathered over to members of the Chester Mountaineering Club, who, for a time, were fired with the same intention. One or two new climbs were discovered at their summer evening haunt of Craig y Forwen during 1974, notably Close to the Edge, but their guidebook aspirations also faded, lacking anyone with sufficient motivation to see it through.

Such a person eventually materialised in the form of Stuart Cathcart, then a student at Chester College, who had opened his account by climbing Digitron with Gerald Swindley in 1973. Next to feel the force of his pioneering energy was Maeshafn Quarry, where the Burgess twins had climbed the fine crack of The Minstrel in 1972. During the next few years, Cathcart, mainly with Swindley or Tom Curtis, 'worked out' the quarry, climbing all the existing routes and adding many new ones. Outstanding amongst these were Mathematical Workout (free) and Running With the Wolf. This activity culminated in 1977 when Cathcart published his guide to Maeshafn, which encouraged considerable interest at the time, but unfortunately took the landowner by surprise. Alarmed by this sudden invasion of his land, he banned access to the crag. However, this problem has now been ironed out, and access will usually be granted on request. (See access notes).

Having cut his teeth on this project Cathcart began to turn virtually all his attention to documenting the rest of Clwyd limestone. The smaller cliffs were methodically 'worked out' in the manner of Maeshafn. In the Eglwyseg Valley fine climbs were found along the length of the escarpment to equal or surpass in quality anything at the popular Craig y Forwen. Go a Go Go, Hungry Days.

10% Special, Mental Transition, Solo in Soho, Sir Cathcart D'Eath, Jibber, Hyper Drive. Raging Storm and Any Which Way, all climbed within the last few years by Cathcart, either solo, or with one of a variety of partners, are representatives of the many superb routes to be sampled on these previously neglected crags.

In contrast to the rapid development of these smaller cliffs, Craig Arthur, the area's centrepiece, has been brought slowly to maturity like a fine wine. Following the ascent of Digitron in 1973, the cliff saw little activity during the next 3 years, though Alan Rouse is reported to have climbed a route in the vicinty of Tito, precise details of which are not known. However, from 1976, the pace of exploration accelerated as the ubiquitous Stuart Cathcart began to fill the gaps. Partnered by Gerald Swindley or Nick Slaney, he climbed the fine steep routes of Fall and Decline, Manikins of **Horror and Swlabr link, plus the Serious Deadly Trap, and in 1978** produced what is probably the most exacting route in this guidebook, Survival of the Fastest, an impending crack and wall requiring a bolt for protection. This exceptional line is as yet unrepeated. During the last 3 years, the desire to complete work on the guide has spurred an even greater output of routes, outstanding amongst which have been Three Dimensions (Cathcart, with Mike Hughes and Frank Bennett), Scary Fairy (with Paul Scott and Frank Bennett), and the dramatic Gates of the Golden Dawn (with Greg Griffiths). Finally, Cathcart's dominance of Eglwyseg pioneering was reinforced as the last major line succumbed. Reacting furtively to the first threat of competition, he co-opted 'Wee Dave' Whitlow to snatch a free ascent of the previously pegged corner and bulge near the left end of the cliff. Le Chacal, a spectacular, though not desperate, piece of climbing, seems destined for classic status.

Meanwhile, the odd gems were still to be found at Craig y Forwen, where the prime testpiece remains the fierce Shooting Star, climbed by Cathcart and Swindley in 1979. High above the ford, in full view of the parking space, two of the finest bits of wall on the crag remained unled until the summer of 1981. In June, Cathcart, with Mal Cameron, climbed the prominent Taerg Wall, a superb pitch with the finest situation on the crag. The following month, as Cathcart's manuscript typing progress made its way along the Upper Tier, the urgency of climbing the 'last great problem' became pressing, and three evenings of concentrated effort were required to produce Vertical Games, the crux move finally made to appreciative cheers from a youth group camping below.

And so, at last, the guide has been completed, almost entirely due to the dedication and enthusiasm of one man. Stuart Cathcart's appeals for information have met with little response, and Andy Pollitt's Calculus at Maeshafn has been the only evidence in recent years of exploratory interest outside his sphere of influence. Other 'last great problems' exist throughout the area, some very hard, others not so. Some have been neglected purely through lack of time and opportunity. Hopefully, this guide will promote an awareness of the wealth of good climbing that Clwyd has to offer, both as a staging post on the way to or from the overrun crags of Snowdonia, and as an area worth visiting purely on its own merit.

GEOLOGY NOTES

The area covered by this guidebook is known as the Vale of Clwyd and the Clwydian Range. The area trends from north to south-east and forms the eastern limb of a synclinal rift valley. There is a clearly marked fault scarp facing west.

Much of the area is overlain by alluvial and glacial deposits which mask the underlying formations.

The formations of the Clwydians are hard and resist erosion which results in this impressive miniature ridge offering wide open views from the summits.

The faulting has left rocks of the Upper Carboniferous Age resting against Silurian formations. (Ludlow or Wenlock Series).

To the south of the area the River Dee has made a breach in the Carboniferous Series. The river which is incised into the Silurian beds appears to have cut down into the later stages of the Quaterniary Ice Age.

To the north of Llangollen there is a wall of Carboniferous Limestone which is resting unconformably on the Lower Palaeozoic beds. Hollows in the beds being filled by red basement beds which are exposed at the foot of the limestone scarp. The limestone beds dip eastwards at an angle of between 5 and 10 degrees. This limestone scarp, which is most prominent in the Eglwyseg Valley, exhibits fine examples of free faces, waxing and waning slopes. There are few examples of features of Karst topography in this area, unlike the Pennines.

TECHNICAL INFORMATION

The area which this guidebook covers comprises cliffs from 40 ft - 150 ft high. This range in the route lengths presents a problem for grading the climbs. It would be unreasonable to give a 40 ft. 'low crag' route an extreme grade of E5, considering that the grade represents the most serious situation attainable in climbing terms. Similarly it would be lunacy to use only technical grades for a serious 'high crag' route.

It is therefore necessary to use a combination of the generally known and accepted system and a slightly modified system to cope with this variety.

For both the 'high' and 'low' crags the standard adjectival grading system has been used up to HVS as follows:

Easy	Mild Severe
Moderate	Severe
Difficult	Hard Severe
Very Difficult	Mild Very Severe
Hard Very Difficult	Very Severe
	Hard Very Severe

The modification of the known system has taken place in the Extreme grade, that meaning above Hard Very Severe. It is no longer sufficient to give a climb just an Extreme grade, as many factors may influence this one category, being the difference from either a straightforward well protected, harmless, Extreme to a modern day horror. Therefore the generally recognised use of an adjectival, open ended E grade is used to represent an overall impression of the difficulty, which includes atmosphere, exposure, protectability and the sustained nature of the route, e.g. E1, E2. E3, E4, etc. The E grading does not denote the technical quality of the route, this is indicated with the use of the open ended numerical system: 4a, 4b, 4c, 5a, 5b, 5c, 6a, 6b, etc. These numerical grades come into operation from the Mild Very Severe upwards.

The 'high crags' in this guidebook (Craig Arthur, Trefor Rocks Quarry and Pantymwyn) will maintain the use of the open ended E grading system for any climb harder than Hard Very Severe, together with a technical numerical grade.

For the 'low crags', (Maeshafn, Pot Hole, Craig y Forwen, The Twilight Crags, Pinfold North and South, Monk's Buttress and Dinbren), a technical grade is used. Also a number scale is used from 1 upwards which indicates *only* the protectability of the route and is in no way an indication as to the ferociousness, looseness or sustained quality of the climb. This will either be highlighted in the relevant text for that climb or be blatantly obvious to the climber viewing from the ground.

For example:

High Crags

Manikins of Horror (Craig Arthur). E2 5c. -

> Overall a well protected route in good surroundings, but technically hard.

Survival of the Fastest. (C Arthur). E4 6b. -

> Overall a route with just enough protection in a way-out situation with technically desperate climbing.

Low Crags

The Minstrel. (Maeshafn). 1. 5b. -

> Overall excellent protection with fairly standard climbing for its grade.

Shooting Star. (Craig y Forwen). 4. 6c. -

> Very poor protection and technically the hardest climbing in the guide.

All the routes have been led and naturally the information given for the 'low crags' is more than adequate. With the new system it at least gives the climber a serious feel of pioneering the ascent even though it may only be short, still relying on the climber's visual judgement prior to the climb as to its character.

Working in conjunction with the new grading system, rope lengths have only been included on 'high crag' routes. On nearly all the 'low crag' routes it is obvious that a single or twin 150ft rope will suffice without any problems.

A star system has been used to indicate the quality of the routes irrespective of the grades or the system. A route is generally excellent in many respects to merit three stars, but the absence of stars does not mean that the climb is unsatisfactory, as poor climbs are specifically described as such.

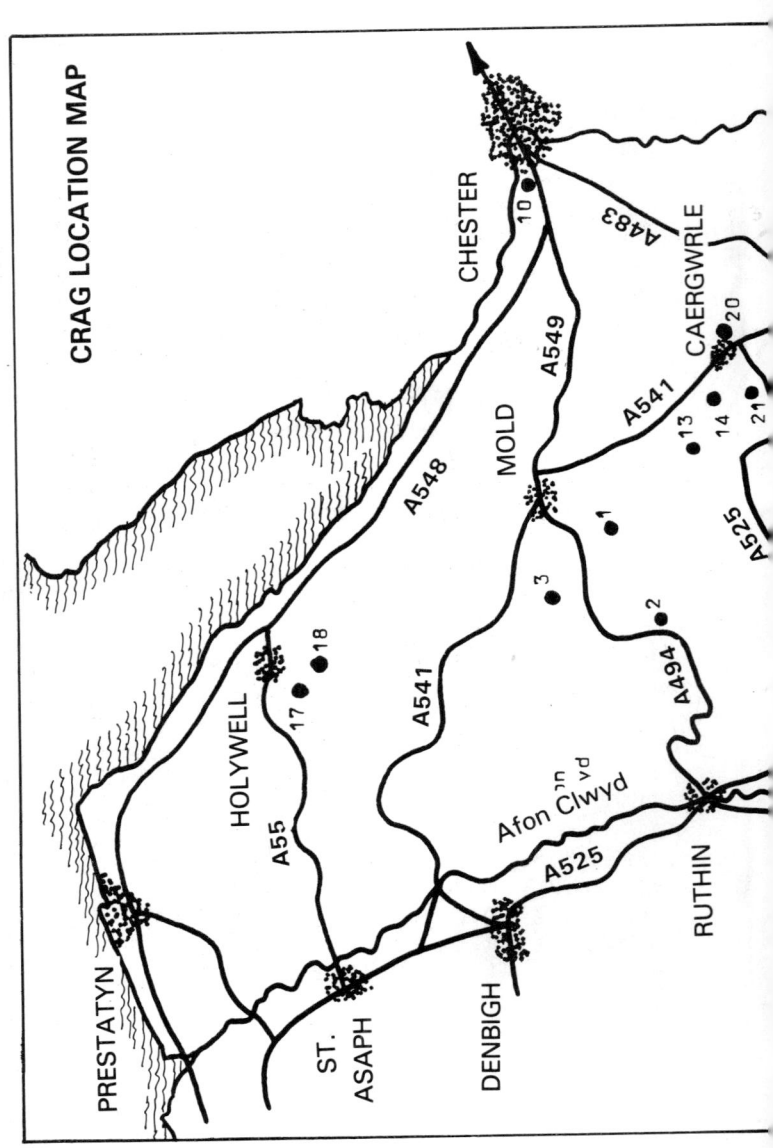

CRAG LOCATION MAP

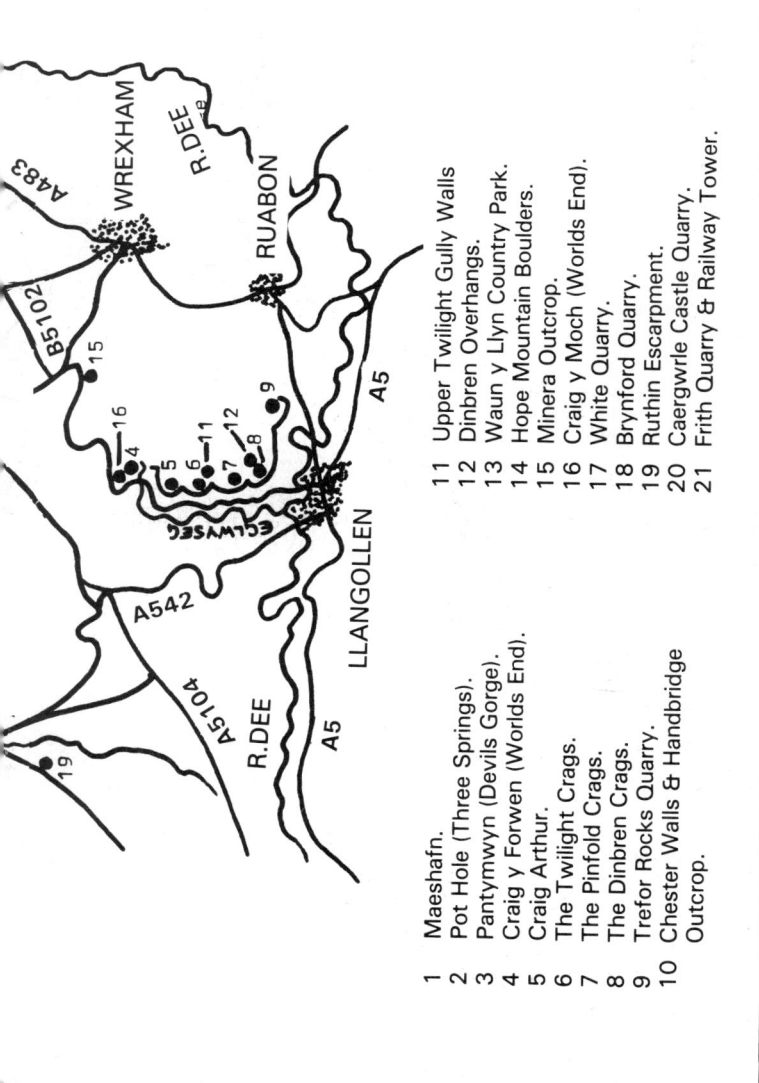

1 Maeshafn.
2 Pot Hole (Three Springs).
3 Pantymwyn (Devils Gorge).
4 Craig y Forwen (Worlds End).
5 Craig Arthur.
6 The Twilight Crags.
7 The Pinfold Crags.
8 The Dinbren Crags.
9 Trefor Rocks Quarry.
10 Chester Walls & Handbridge
   Outcrop.
11 Upper Twilight Gully Walls
12 Dinbren Overhangs.
13 Waun y Llyn Country Park.
14 Hope Mountain Boulders.
15 Minera Outcrop.
16 Craig y Moch (Worlds End).
17 White Quarry.
18 Brynford Quarry.
19 Ruthin Escarpment.
20 Caergwrle Castle Quarry.
21 Frith Quarry & Railway Tower.

MAESHAFN

OS. Ref 214615.   OS Sheet No. 117. 1:50,000.

SITUATION

This old limestone quarry is situated 3 miles due south-west of the centre of Mold, almost completely hidden until within a few hundred yards of the rock. The quarry is more than ideally situated for passing climbers on their way to and from North Wales and the northern cities via the A494(T) Mold to Ruthin road. Its situation also guarantees a certain amount of good weather when more western districts have poor prevailing conditions.

The entrance to the quarry is reached by turning off the main A494 (T) road at the top of the long hill out of Mold and very near to the Rainbow Inn, heading east up a steep lane from the Rainbow Garage. This lane is followed for a mile to a T-junction with the Owain Glyndwr Hotel pub on the corner, turn right here and follow the lane to the first farm on the left after a quarter of a mile MR.214613, Bryngwyn Farm. The crag lies up a gated track from a bungalow opposite the farm. *SEE ACCESS NOTES*.

Parking and Approach

Cars must not be driven from the farm buildings up the track to the quarry, but should be left on the grass verge near where the track starts in the lane and not too close to the bungalow or farm as to disturb the residents.

Follow the gated track uphill past a site office building for 300 yards into the quarry. If the track is followed right into the quarry one ends up in the White Wall Area. If the track is left and the open field is crossed, after passing through the first gate by the site office, then one comes straight into the Main Wall Area with the White Wall Area along to the left and The Amphitheatre to the right, facing the crag.

Access

Important Must Be Read. The quarry lies on land owned by Mr. W. Thomas of Bryngwyn Farm at the start of the track. He may be willing to allow climbers, in small numbers to use the quarry, ONLY IF PERMISSION IS SOUGHT. This step MUST be taken in order to avoid a firm request to leave, as climbers can be seen from the farm. The access situation here is very delicate and we must do

16

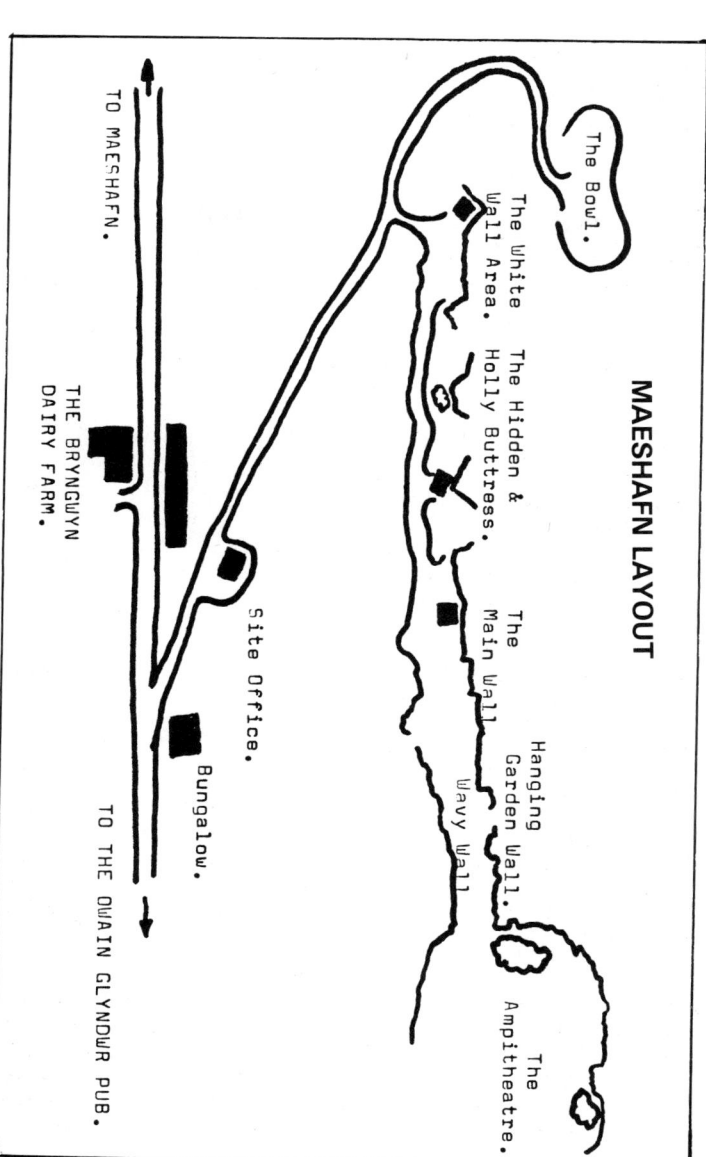

MAESHAFN LAYOUT

The Bowl.

The White
Wall Area.

The Hidden &
Holly Buttress.

The
Main Wall

Hanging
Garden Wall.

Wavy Wall

The
Ampitheatre.

TO MAESHAFN.

THE BRYNGWYN
DAIRY FARM.

Site Office.

Bungalow.

TO THE OWAIN GLYNDWR PUB.

17

nothing to disturb it. Mr Thomas is by no means against climbers, he understandably only wishes to protect his land, and therefore on no account should an aggressive attitude be taken if one is refused permission on certain days.

Character and Layout

The quarry is approximately 100 years old and has been climbed on for some time by local climbers and so there is actually very little loose rock or large amounts of vegetation on any of the routes. Being west facing the rock dries very quickly and is an attractive proposition on summer evenings and is regularly visited by climbers during the winter months. Unlike many quarries it does have a very pleasant atmosphere not dissimilar to an escarpment crag, as there are fine views from almost anywhere in the quarry out over the Alyn Valley to Moel Fammau.

The quarry is split into three basic areas with smaller buttresses between and a separate small quarry at the northern end. The directions are given facing the rock with the layout, as follows. Starting at the extreme righthand end (southern) of the quarry, (the quarry is an open cast type and so is a long wall rather than a hole in the ground), there is a large enclosed area of walls with the fitting name THE AMPHITHEATRE

Walking north out of The Amphitheatre (left) one passes immediately through a small gorge with a larger right wall half covered in hanging vegetation, HANGING GARDEN WALL, with the short unusually formed WAVY WALL just beyond.

From now onwards the walls are less enclosed having in general only a low earth bank opposite. This change in surroundings also marks the start of the MAIN WALL AREA. This is probably the most popular and certainly the largest expanse of rock, with steep walls and ferocious cracks. The three most popular and classic routes on the crag, The Minstrel, Mathematical Workout and the Corner, climb the central section of this wall.

Leaving the Main Wall Area at the northern end by the first of the steel containers continue along the dirt track to another steel container with a small buttress tucked away behind, THE HIDDEN BUTTRESS. A short way beyond this is another small more open buttress with a large holly bush in front of it, THE HOLLY BUTTRESS.

A short way past The Holly Buttress you enter the WHITE WALL AREA which just ranks as the highest piece of rock in the quarry at

85 feet. With very few good crack lines to follow, apart from on the righthand side, the climbing is generally bold and committing up the steep walls with Running With The Wolf ranking as probably the best route in the quarry and certainly high in the bold category, with the girdle being a close contender.

The last small piece of rock is in a rather depressing situation, literally in a hole in the ground, THE BOWL, but does however, have two out of three very worthwhile solo routes up good slabby rock over roofs. This area can be reached by continuing up the track which is followed from the farm around the back of the White Wall Area or by walking over the top from the White Wall. The slabs and roof which the routes climb are fairly obvious down at the bottom of the rubbish filled bowl.

The Climbs

Facing the rock the climbs are described from right to left starting in The Amphitheatre on the righthand wall at a large almost fully grown ash tree.

THE AMPHITHEATRE

1. **ASH TREE SCRAMBLE**   Diff.
   Climb the cracks and blocks up to and above the large ash tree.

2. **WANDERER**   Mild VS
   4c. Climb a corner 5ft left of the large ash tree until a smaller ash tree is reached and traverse out left across the steep wall to the grass terrace as for the finish of Shattered Crack.

3. **THE ARÊTE**   HVS
   5b. The left arête of the narrow steep slab to a good ledge at 20ft, or climb the slab direct over the bulge. Move directly up the wall above crossing Wanderer to a slightly loose finish. A good interesting start.

4. **SHATTERED CRACK**   Mild Severe**
   Climb easily up the obvious crack to step left onto a ledge just above the steep section and on up to the grass terrace. A steep classic.

5. **THE BULGER**   1**
   5b. An excellent testpiece with good protection. Start just left of Shattered Crack at a righthand leaning corner and arête. Climb the corner and steep slab to the bulging wall and crack just left of the top section of Shattered Crack.

6. **LITTLE FINGER JAM**   HVS
   5a. Start below the small overhang at 5ft on the steep slab wall.

Pull over the overhang to climb a thin crack direct to the grass terrace.

7. SLING   H Severe

The obvious flake crack to an old peg and sling near the top, passing this to finish on the grass terrace. A nice route.

8. ELEPHANT CRACK   Severe

Left of Sling is a vegetated groove with a large tree on the left. Climb the groove to the large overhang and up the large body chimney finishing on the left.

9. RAM JAM   2

5c. Although only a few very hard moves with good protection they are performed in a superb position over the overhang. Start as for Elephant Crack and climb to the large overhang, move left across the slab below it to beneath an obvious finger-crack splitting the roof. Climb this ferocious finger-crack on good jams.

To the left of Ram Jam is a large cave with a heavily vegetated easy angled wall above and to the left of it. The next seven climbs are to be found on the steep and overhanging walls to the left of this vegetation.

10. LABIANUS   VS

4a. Start at the foot of a short steep wall at the extreme right-hand side of the walls near to the obvious left facing steep slab. Gain the foot of the slab and climb up out rightwards to the edge and follow this to the top.

11. JUST JOLLY   VS

4b. The steep main wall is cut from top to bottom by a shattered crack. Climb the crack for a few feet to a large ledge move right and up to the old peg in the wall passing this to gain the easy groove near its top. Finish up the groove.

12. VULCER   HVS

5a. Climb the steep shattered crack which splits the wall from top to bottom starting as for JUST JOLLY. A strenuous route with a slightly loose finish.

13. ITSU   3*

5b. Climb the thin crack and corner 5ft left of Vulcer from the large ledge a few feet up that route. A serious bold route.

14. THE RASP   3*

5c. A very strenuous and cutting climb which is also difficult to protect. The wall to the left of Vulcer is undercut on the right side of this and is an obvious protruding spike with a slot above in the lip of the overhang. Climb direct to the spike and using the slot pull over onto the slab above, continue up diagonally left.

15. **BLUE CHROME**   HVS
5a +. Climb the protecting flakes and blocks just left of The Rasp to make a difficult step right onto the easier slab which is followed up leftwards to the top.

16. **GORILLA WALTZ**   VS
4b. Climb the overhanging groove up out of the lefthand end of the undercut, use the tree in a gorilla fashion to continue to the top.

The next four climbs are on the slabby wall left of the over-grown right wall as one leaves The Amphitheatre through a small gorge, towards the Main Wall Area. On the left of this half-vegetated wall is a separate small wavy buttress, one of the four climbs takes the obvious crack up this.

HANGING GARDEN WALLS

17. **GARDEN WALL 1**   VS
4b. A large pinnacle flake dominates the lower wall just left of the hanging vegetated wall, start on the right of the flake. Climb the steep wall and open groove to the top of the flake, step right and up to the top.

18. **GARDEN WALL 2**   VS
4c. Climb the short slab on the left of the pinnacle flake with a difficult step left onto the upper slab and the top.

19. **GARDEN WALL 3**   VS
4b The steep crack in the short wall left of the pinnacle flake is followed until a difficult pull onto the slab is made and up to the top.

20. **WAVY WALL**   H Severe
On the separate short buttress with large horizontal waves or ripples 20ft left of the Garden Wall routes. Climb the obvious crack up the waves to the top, interesting.

Left of the small buttress which Wavy Wall climbs there is a steep grass slope which is used as a descent. Left again is the start of the Main Wall Area with its excellent steep walls, arêtes and corners offering some of the best climbing at Maeshafn, often technical and strenuous. The climbs start at the extreme righthand end of the walls at a steep slab.

THE MAIN WALL AREA

21. **SLIP**   H Severe
Climb the steep slab which slants up to the right from a small cave. The start is more awkward than it appears.

22. **FORMIDABLE**   VS
4c. Climb the dubious looking arête which marks the start of the steep main walls proper and on the left of the small cave. Short but sharp.

23. **PENGRAIL**   1
5b+. Start 5ft left of Formidable at a shattered crack. Climb the steep wall up the crack slanting rightwards with a hard move halfway.

24. **BAROUCHE**   2*
5b. A steep route with just enough protection. Start on the right of the flat topped flake with a wild rose bush. Climb the thin crack up rightwards until it is possible to step left to a small ledge with a very small tree. With increasing difficulty move right and up the thin crack to good holds at the top in a stepped niche.

25. **KNOTTY PROBLEM**   HVS*
5a+. Fine climbing. Start on the front of the flat topped flake with the wild rose bush growing from its top. Gain the top of the flake and the smaller mantleshelf ledge above, continue up the thin crack above, technical.

26. **LAXIX**   4**
5c. An extremely bold and sustained route. 10ft left of the start of Knotty Problem is an old rightward trending peg crack, start just right of this. Climb the steep wall on small friable holds joining the peg crack at 15ft, continue up the crack to a good sharp flake edge and the top.

27. **THE SECRET**   3
5c. Climb the slightly overhanging wall to a good hold and the footholds on the traverse on The Corner route, starting 8ft right of that route. Move left along the traverse in reverse to the peg in the corner itself and finish straight up passing the old peg, a difficult finish.

28. **THE CORNER**   HVS***
5a. Climb the obvious corner and swing up around the small roof at 15ft and up to the old peg. Traverse right with difficulty to a good footledge and up more easily to the top. A classic.

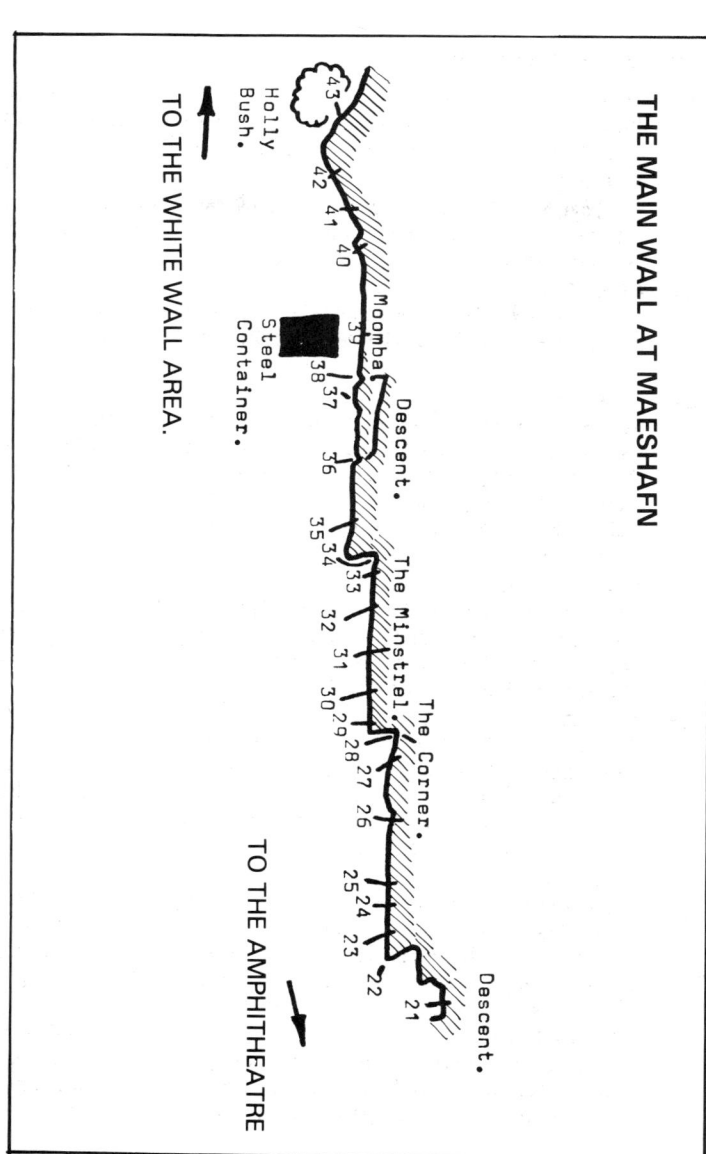

THE MAIN WALL AT MAESHAFN

TO THE WHITE WALL AREA.

Holly Bush.

Steel Container.

Moomba.

Descent.

The Minstrel.

The Corner.

TO THE AMPHITHEATRE

Descent.

29. **CALCULUS** 3**

6a. An interesting route which connects the top arête, originally Esoteric, with the lower easier arête by a technical move over the small roof. Start at the foot of the arête on the left of The Corner. Climb the steep arête to the overhang and several good runners, pull over the roof by a good flake and continue more easily to the top staying close to the arête.

30. **MATHEMATICAL WORKOUT** 3***

6a. One of the hardest routes at Maeshafn with reasonably good protection on small wires. Start 6ft left of The Corner below a well pegged crack with the name Blood Climb scratched on the rock. Climb the crack to the small overhang and continue with great difficulty over the roof to a small but excellent arête hold and more easily up the slab above.

31. **THE MINSTREL** 1**

5b. An enjoyable well protected route. Climb the steep finger crack just left of Mathematical Workout with a hard move over the bulge at half height to gain the easier crack above. Finish directly over the overhang above to the top.

32. **ROYAL PLUME** 1

6a Start at the foot of the thin crack left of the start of The Minstrel. Climb the crack to the overhang, move up and with difficulty gain the upper slab slightly right. Move back left across the slab and up to the top.

33. **FLYING BLOC** 1

5a+. Climb the last of the four cracks up the steep wall starting at the foot of the crack left of the Royal Plume to the overhang. Climb the overhang and on up the easier wall above on the left.

34. **ANCILLARY** Severe

The obvious vegetated groove to the Ash tree and the short wall behind the tree.

35. **YOBO** H Severe

Tp the left of the vegetated groove of Ancillary is an easier angled section of slabs. Climb the cracks and large holds straight up the right side of these slabs to finish a few feet left of Ancillary.

36. **RAMBLER** V Diff

Climb the vegetated groove and wall in the centre of the slabby area. Often used as a descent.

37. **LAYBACK ON ME** H Severe
15ft left of Rambler is an obvious righthand trending line of overhangs. Follow this line to the easy terrace on Rambler and up to the top.

38. **APEX** 1*
5b. A testing problem. The slabs verge into a steep wall just right of a steel container. Climb up into a short but steep groove at the start of the walls to a small thorn bush, move below this to the right and up easily to the top.

39. **MOOMBA** 4
6a + . Start 10ft left of Apex behind the steel container. Climb straight up and step left onto a small hold, move up the steep wall slightly right to better holds and the top, poorly protected.

40. **JOCCA** HVS
5a + . The steep walls merge into easier slabs at a short steep once undercut slab. Gain this steep slab on its right and climb the delicate crack to the top.

41. **THRUTCH** H Severe
Start on the right of the small promentary left of Jocca. Pull over the overhang and bulge onto the slab and continue up more easily to join Jocca near the top.

42. **JOKER** V Diff.
Start a few feet left of Thrutch on the front of the promentary. Climb easily up the steep wall on large holds and up the easy slab to the top.

43. **HOLLY TREE WALL** VS
4. A line of holds ascend up leftwards around the top of the holly tree. Follow these to the finish up the slab. A fine little route.

MAIN WALL GIRDLE 3
An excellent girdle with some 300ft of sustained climbing and with minimal protection on most of the more difficult sections.

Pitch 1. 5c. Start for Jocca at the foot of the steep slab. Climb to the top of the slab, move up and out right to descend slightly to a small ledge. Follow the horizontal crack line rightwards with difficulty to the easier ground. Move right swinging around the arête to belay above the thorn bush on Apex.

Pitch 2. 4a. Traverse easily along the terraces and upper slab on Yobo to the Ash tree and a belay.

Pitch 3. 5b. Move up right from the tree across a slab to below the overhang on The Minstrel. Traverse across the steep slab, excellent, to the right, to swing around the arête near the top to large ledges at the top of The Corner, poor belay.

Pitch 4. 5c. A demanding pitch. Descend to the small ledge at the end of the traverse on The Corner. Traverse right from here with great difficulty past a peg runner on Laxix to gain another small ledge and down slightly to the mantleshelf ledge on Knotty Problem. Move across the steep wall to finish up the thin crack at the top of Barouche. A difficult and worrying pitch for the second.

Walking north, to the left, from the Main Wall Area along the track towards the White Wall Area one passes two small buttresses set back behind a screen of bushes. the first is the Hidden Buttress found lurking behind one of the large steel containers, a little further on is the Holly Bush Buttress which is the more climbed on of the two.

THE HIDDEN & HOLLY BUTTRESSES

44. SITA   2
5c. On the Hidden Buttress starting on the left of the obvious sharp arête. Using a large pocket on the left of the arête pull up to a large ledge on the arête, continue up across the left wall to the top.

45. WILKINSON SWORD EDGE   VS
4c. On the Holly Buttress starting on the right of the large holly bush. Climb the sharp arête mainly on its right side.

46. HOLLY BUSH WALL   V Diff.
Start on the right of the holly bush and climb up across the top of the wall above the bush and then direct to the top.

47. MAEVE   3*
6a. Start on the left of the holly bush. Climb up diagonally rightwards to above the holly on poor rounded holds and up to the top. A difficult technical and poorly protected route.

48. TWIN PINS   H Severe
Climb the twin cracks up the slabby wall left of the holly bush.

A very short way beyond the Hidden and Holly Buttreses where the track opens out into a cul-de-sac is the White Wall Area. Starting on the extreme righthand side of these walls behind a small thorn bush.

THE WHITE WALL AREA

49. GANTREE — H Severe

From behind the small thorn bush climb the small slabs and overhangs on good holds to a large ledge on the arête, up the short wall to the top.

50. CARROLL STREET — HVS

5a. Start 5ft left of Gantree. Up the obvious traverse line leftwards into the corner, climb around the overhangs to the right, delicate, to finish up the short but slightly loose wall.

51. ODYSSEUS — HVS**

5a A fine short route. Climb direct to the short corner on Carroll Street from a shorter corner on the left, delicate. Climb the corner and traverse out left swinging onto the steep wall which is climbed direct to the top.

52. WHITE SPRING — H Severe

Climb the obvious shallow groove and cracks left of Odysseus to the top.

53. RUNNING WITH THE WOLF — 4***

5c. One of the best routes in the quarry, both technical and bold. The steep walls left of White Spring have a small overhang running across them in the upper half, start below these on the left of a prominent arête of rock capped by a wild rose bush. Climb the steep lower walls on friable pockets trending leftwards to a good resting ledge and a poor runner low down. Move up with increasing difficulty rightwards to a good peg runner below the small overhang. Step right with difficulty to a good flake crack above which is followed to the top.

54. MUSLIM — HVS

5a Start at a thin crack some 20ft left of the start of Running with the Wolf. Climb the crack to a ledge and up the steep slab and short corner which marks the left-hand end of the line of overhangs.

55. RAMA — H Severe

Start as for Muslim. Climb the crack to the ledge and up the slab to the left to the top.

56. FLOTTA ARÊTE — V Diff

The steep walls end on the left with a rounded arête. Start on left of the arête, traverse up right onto the arête and follow it to the top.

57. CYCLOPS   HVS
    5b. Start as for Flotta Arête. Climb the thin crack in the
    slightly bulging wall direct to the top, strenuous.

58. HACO   4**
    5a. Not technically hard but poorly protected. Start as for
    Cyclops and follow a line of 'knobbles and stuck on flakes' up
    left-wards to a good resting ledge, traverse right for 5ft and up
    the short bulging wall.

59. HOT TIN ROOF   3
    6a. Hard technical and strenuous moves throughout. Start on
    top of the steel container. Climb the thin crack in the steep wall
    to the top.

60. EL CID   H Severe
    Climb the obvious poor corner behind the steel container with
    an awkward step left at the top. A poor route.

WHITE WALL TRAVERSE   3
Pitch 1.   5c. Start as for Hot Tin Roof on top of the steel container.
    Climb the steep thin crack as for Hot Tin Roof to half height
    and make a difficult traverse right to the resting ledge on Haco,
    move right to easier climbing and the rounded arête and a belay
    on the right.

Pitch 2.   5b + . Traverse easily right along the ledge below the small
    overhang to the peg runner on Running with the Wolf. Move
    right until it is possible to clip a peg and make a short tension
    move to gain the groove of White Spring and a poor belay.

Pitch 3.   4c. Continue on a similar line along small ledges to make a
    reverse move down around the overhang on Carroll Street
    following below it to the ledge on the far arête.
    A good route with a serious first pitch.

Following the track out of the White Wall Area on to the main
access track, turn right and follow it around to behind the White
Wall Area and a cul-de-sac rubbish dump. There is a large amount of
rock here but a large portion of it is very loose except for the lowest
hole in the quarry which is known as The Bowl. There are only three
routes or problems worth mentioning, two which take the smooth
slabs and overhang and one which takes the smaller slabs and
overhangs, which are a little loose, on the immediate left.

61. REACH   VS*
    4c. Start in the centre of the smooth slab and overhang section.
    Climb the slab and pull over the overhang on good but rounded

holds at the break in the slab which is above the overhang.

62. PULL   VS*
    4c – Climb the slab and overhang near the left end of the
    smooth slabs.

63. AND OVER   VS +
    5a. Start on the left of the large pile of rocks. Climb the slabby
    wall and up around the overhangs to a short slab and the top.

POT HOLE QUARRY (THREE SPRINGS)

OS. Ref. 192597   O.S. Sheet No. 116. 1:50.000

Situation

This small quarry lies amongst trees in a very pleasant side valley off
the River Alun Valley and approximately half a mile south of the
village of Llanferres.

Parking and Approach

Parking is in a large lay-by on the left side of the A494 coming from
Mold towards Ruthin, half a mile south of the village of Llanferres.
The top of the quarry is visible from the lay-by looking east.

To reach the quarry, walk back 100 yards from the lay-by towards
Llanferres (north), to a marked footpath and stile across the field to
a footbridge across the River Alun. After crossing the bridge follow
the bank upstream to a tributary stream which is followed to a stile,
the quarry is on the left a further 100 yards up the track beyond the
stile.

IT IS IMPORTANT THAT THE CORRECT APPROACH IS
FOLLOWED OR ACCESS ACROSS THIS VALUABLE FARM—
LAND WILL OTHERWISE BE PROHIBITED.

Access

The quarry appears to be situated on common land but is in fact
owned by the farm across the road from the parking lay-by. As yet
the farmer has shown no objection to the use of the quarry as long as
the correct approach is taken and do not leave litter.

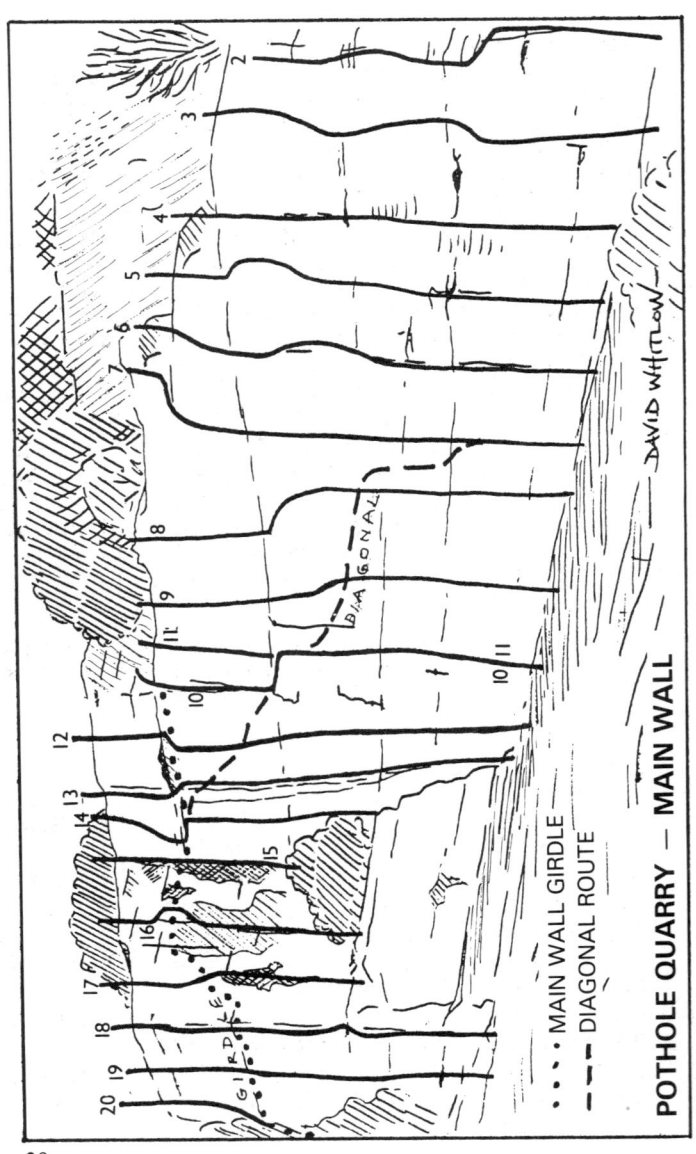

POTHOLE QUARRY — MAIN WALL

· · · · · MAIN WALL GIRDLE
— — — DIAGONAL ROUTE

30

Character and Layout

Even though this is a minor cliff the climbing is of a fine quality on excellent rock with good protection on most routes or nearby belays at the top for top-roping. The rock on the Main Wall is uncharacteristically solid for a quarry, where most of the climbing is on pockets and large rugosities. The Side Wall appears a little loose but once tackled proves to be fairly solid.

The quarry is divided into two, The Main Wall and The Side Wall. The Main Wall is the largest and highest expanse of rock, approximately 200 feet long and 70 feet at its highest tapering down rightwards from an obvious square cut corner, The Right Angle. Left of this is a slightly overhanging wall with a chamfered arête on its left. Talking Fingers takes the overhanging wall. Right of the corner of The Right Angle is a twin crack splitting the wall at its highest, The Dog, and on the steep wall between the two is Right Wall.

The side wall is low down to the left of the Main Wall. This rather broken short face contains several interesting lines of a very steep nature. The most obvious feature is a small overhang near the top on the right side with a crack splitting it and the wall below. This is taken by Cima. No pitch lengths have been included as 150 feet of rope is more than adequate on all climbs described.

The Climbs

Facing The Main Wall, the far right-hand end tapers down in steps to a blunt arête left of a sycamore tree. The routes are desribed from left to right.

THE MAIN WALL

1.   MESTRE   Severe
   The obvious crack right of the blunt arête.

2.   SESTO   V. Diff.
   The blunt arête starting on the right and finishing on the left.

3.   SELVA   VS
   4a. The thin crack and steep wall 5ft left of the blunt arête behind the larger of two thorn bushes.

4.   CRISTALLO   H Severe
   The direct vertical crack up between two white marks.

5.   MURREN   H Severe
   The middle of three finger cracks left of the thorn bush, gain a scoop to finish.

6. **THE WATZMANN** VS
   4b. The left-hand of three cracks with a difficult finish.

7. **UN-AIDED** VS
   4b. The thin crack with its name scratched at the foot of the climb.

8. **GRIZZLY** VS
   4c. Just left of Un-Aided a very thin crack is followed to the top finishing as for Un-Aided. AFS scratched on the rock at the start.

9. **MAJOR** HVS
   5a. 3ft left of Grizzly following a thin crack which stops at 10ft. and starts again 10ft higher above a blank wall.

10. **VETTA** VS**
    5a. A thin crack just right of the tree stump leads to a ledge below a blank wall. Step left on to the smooth wall to climb the excellent crack to the terrace.

11. **VETTA VARIATION** 3**
    5c. From the ledge at half height on Vetta continue directly up the wall above, good climbing but poorly protected.

12. **CEBA** 1**
    5a. The crack behind the tree stump with hard moves over the small overhang.

13. **THE DOG** 1***
    5b. Climb the single and then the twin cracks either direct or on the pocketed right wall at half height. A superb short route.

14. **RIGHT WALL** 3***
    5c. Start on the right edge of the corner terrace just left of The Dog. Hard climbing leads to a thin crack at 15ft via pockets, slightly higher is a good runner before a horizontal break is reached at 30ft. Move left along the break and up more easily to the top. Good finger exercises.

15. **THE RIGHT ANGLE** H Severe
    The obvious awkward corner.

16. **TALKINGFINGERS** 1*
    5c. Climb the thin yellow finger crack 8ft left of The Right Angle, hard at the top moving right slightly. Very well protected and very steep.

17. **TALKING LEGS** 2.
    5c. Gain a ledge, off balance, just left of Talking Fingers, then the overhanging wall above.

18. **EPITAPH** VS
4c. Climb the arête starting low down at the foot of a thin crack on the left wall. A pleasant climb.

19. **DROGGO** VS
4a. The obvious crack in the wall left of the arête of Epitaph.

20. **MANGO** H Severe
The crack and groove to the top behind the ash tree, difficult finish.

21. **OWL WALL** Severe
The wall climbing up diagonally right starting on the left of the ash and sycamore trees.

DIAGONAL ROUTE 110 feet 1***
A superb route climbing right to left up across The Main Wall taking in some of the best climbing from several good routes.

5a. Start as for Un-Aided and climbing it for 8ft to traverse left with feet on the horizontal break to the crack line of Vetta, up this to the smooth wall. Move up and across to the small overhang on Cebo, continue left across The Dog and along the horizontal break as for Right Wall finishing up the route.

MAIN WALL GIRDLE 150 feet 2
Pitch 1. 100ft. 5c. Start as for Mango for 10ft to an obvious traverse line which is followed for 60ft to the orange coloured ledge on Epitaph. Using a high pocket on the steep right wall of the arête, gain the larger ledge above with difficulty. Move up and traverse right with increasing difficulty into The Right Angle corner. Belay at the top of the corner.
Pitch 2. 50ft. 5a. Move down 10ft and follow the obvious horizontal traverse line across the main walls finishing on the terrace as for Vetta.

THE SIDE WALL
Facing The Side Wall, the routes are described from right to left.

22. **CIMA** HVS*
5a. A finger crack splits the wall and main overhang on the right-hand side of the face, this is followed to the top.

23. **TOSA** 1*
5a. Left of Cima is a white overhanging wall which leads to a small ledge then the easier crack on the wall above. Strenuous.

24. BURNING BUSH   VS
    4c. The steep arête on large holds to the small bush and the
    shallow groove above to the top.
25. BLINDFOLD   HS
    The obvious corner and wall just to the left of Burning Bush.
26. SUNSET   V Diff.
    The loose crack and short wall 10ft left of Blindfold.

PANTYMWYN (DEVIL'S GORGE)
OS. Ref. 189643   O.S. Sheet No. 116. 1:50,000

Situation
The gorge is marked on the Ordnance Survey map as a 'cave'. The
cave and gorge actually lies on the east bank of the River Alun
amongst the trees. Approach to the gorge can either be by a pleasant
tourist path along the bank of the river or by an easy, quick
approach path from a nearby public road.

Parking and Approach
Either park by the Loggerheads Inn MR. 199626 on the main A494
Mold to Ruthin road, and follow the east bank path downstream for
approximately 2 miles to the gorge.

  Or better, park at the roadside near the T - junction at the west end
of the village of Pantymwyn MR. 192646. Follow a farm access road
downhill (west), signposted as a Public Footpath, through a gate
marked 'Private road no entry' to the bottom of the hill leaving the
track here at a bend and continue straight on to cross a stile. Follow
the path through trees for 50 yards to where the gorge comes dramatically into view down to the right.

Access
The land and the narrow strip of land which the gorge and river lie
on is owned by the Crosville Bus Company and as yet seems
unrestricted. When approaching via the shortest route from
Pantymwyn village one is crossing valuable farm land and naturally
the country code and common sense must apply stringently.

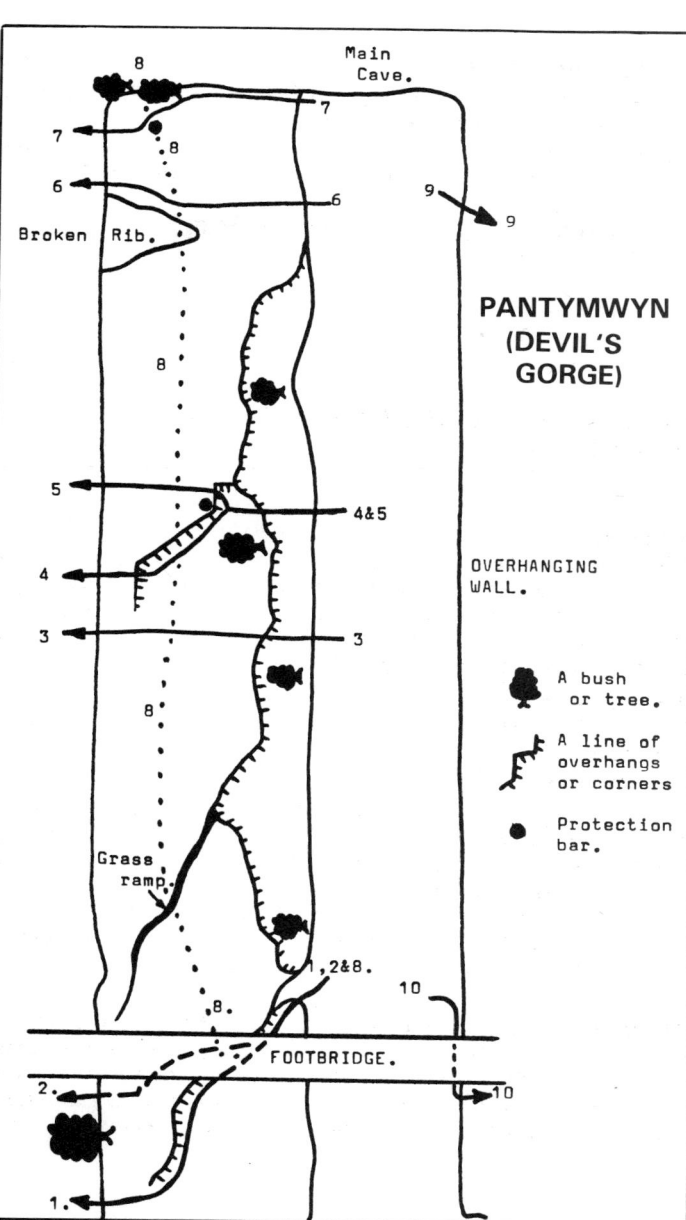

Character and Layout

This is a very impressive piece of rock on first encounters, with one side of this narrow deep gorge dramatically overhanging for its full height of 120ft and the other side complementing it with steep almost featureless slabs. The slabs contain some interesting and at times almost unprotected free routes on perfect rock. An iron footbridge spans the gorge and from here one can view most of the routes with ease and this also makes a superb vantage point for taking photographs.

Opposite on the overhanging wall a line of bolts, now nearly all completely rotten, lead directly up out of the oppressive depths of the gorge to the pleasant wood on the rim with views of the nearby Moel Fammau. The only free route to actually climb the overhanging wall, so far, takes an evasive line up below the footbridge with little protection.

Many of the free routes on the slab are slight eliminates, but in their own right they contain very separate qualities which undoubtedly make them worth climbing, especially as a lead.

The Climbs

On the slab side directly below the footbridge, the routes are described from left to right in a clockwise direction around the gorge.

1. **LADYWRITER** H Severe
    110ft.   Start directly below the footbridge at a deep cut groove on the slab side of the gorge. Climb the groove and continue up broken cracks leftwards to the top edge of the slab left of the bush.

2. **PORTOBELLO BELLE** H Severe
    110ft.   Start as for Ladywriter. Climb to the top of the groove and continue up the overlaps above, up the slab directly below the footbridge to exit on the left.

3. **SINGLE HANDED SAILOR** HVS*
    120ft.   4c.   20ft right of the groove of Ladywriter climb direct to the top passing between two bushes at 15ft and 20ft, poorly protected.

4. **FOLLOW ME HOME** E1**
    120ft.   5a.   Start in the centre of the slab side of the gorge below the protection bar which is at the foot of the leftward slanting overhang and corner up the top half of the slab. Up to the protection bar and follow the slanting overhang and corner

very closely to the top. An excellent route if one follows the slanting overhang properly.

5. **ANGEL OF MERCY**   E2**
120ft.   5a. As for Follow Me Home to the protection bar, step right and climb the overlap and the slab direct to the top avoiding the larger holds on the left. A bold route.

6. **NEWS**   VS
120ft.   4b. Starting 10ft left of the corner at the extreme right-hand side of the slab. Climb straight up to the right side of the broken rib near the top, up on the right of this.

7. **WHERE WE GOING**   H. Severe
120ft.   4b. Climb the corner at the extreme right-hand side of the slab, move onto the slab at the first tree and up it to the top.

8. **GREAT SLAB GIRDLE**   HVS
150ft.   5a. Climb Portobello Belle to the foot of the upper slab and traverse right up for 110ft across the slabs to the trees in the far corner. A poorly protected central section but on good rock.

9. **ROTTEN AID**   A3
120ft. Climb the main overhanging wall 20ft out from the cave entrance. Nearly all the bolts need replacing.

10. **COMMUNIQUE**   5*
75ft.   5b+. Start at the foot of the rightward slanting ramp below the bridge on the overhanging wall side. Follow the ramp on undercuts for 20ft until a long reach is made to a good hold, continue up to a resting ledge. Climb the thin crack above to the large block and the right side of the foot-bridge. A very steep committing route with no real protection.

THE EGLWYSEG VALLEY
O.S. Ref.220473.   O.S. Sheet No. 117. 1:50,000

Situation and Approach
Running north for four and a half miles from behind the ruins of
Castell Dinas Bran, north of Llangollen, there is a magnificent Carboniferous limestone escarpment. This lengthy escarpment over-
looking the Eglwyseg Glen, is easily reached either by the moors road
from Minera and Coedpoeth in the north-east, or very easily from the
main A5 trunk road in Llangollen. A well maintained public lane
runs the full length of the valley, but being very narrow it becomes
somewhat congested on bank holidays and summer Sundays,
although an early start will in general avoid this problem.

Approaching the valley from Llangollen, come over the River Dee
bridge from the A5, which is on the south side, turn right and
immediately left up a steep lane. Continue following the lane
gradually uphill for 2 miles into the Eglwyseg Valley itself marked by
the reaching of a T-junction with the Dinbren Crags up in front
above screes. MR. 317446. To the right is the Panorama road leading
below the Dinbren Crags and along to Trevor Rocks. After a few
hundred yards, if one turns left at the T-junction, the whole
escarpment, except for Worlds End which is obscured by Craig
Arthur, come into splendid view.

Crag Locations
The Eglwyseg Valley must be able to boast one of the finest
collections of varied cliffs on one escarpment in the north-west if not
further afield. For the whole of the four miles of this tributary valley
of the River Dee there is a crag and a possible route to be climbed. It
will undoubtedly be years before the valley reaches full maturity in
climbing terms, but the aim of this guide is to bring to the forefront
the main bulk of good cliffs and the best routes climbed so far.

The escarpment is cut into by four very prominent smaller
tributary valleys. The main climbing is to be found either deep in the
back of these valleys or high up on the promontories between in fine
positions.

As with every good story and in this case, valley, it is best to start at
the beginning, at the head of the valley with Craig y Forwen, better
known to many as 'Worlds End' MR. 234478. Continuing south
down the lane from the ford at Worlds End for three quarters of a

◁ *Craig Arthur Girdle. Climber, Mal Cameron*   39

mile, the most impressive section of cliffs in the valley comes blatantly into view above a pine forest, this is Craig Arthur. MR. 224471. On again around blind bends and narrow descents one soon sees the broken towers on a prominent skyline buttress high above steep screes and marking the first of the smaller tributary valleys, on its right, these are the Eglwyseg Tower crags. MR. 224463. Level with this narrow side valley the road forks at a farm and hump-backed bridge. The right-hand fork climbs steeply up to the Horseshoe Pass by the old road. The left-hand fork leads up to a small church, from here the Pinfold Crags (Rock Farm), North and Monks Buttresses can be seen, with the south buttress only coming into view as one nears Rock Farm itself. Again the lane forks half a mile further on past Rock Farm in a sharp dip. Right is Llangollen, straight on a few hundred yards are the Dinbren Crags in a very small scree filled valley on the left. Continuing along this lane (Panorama Road), for another two miles past two more right forks and the road swings left into a narrow little valley with a sharp hairpin bend, the Trevor Rocks Quarry can easily be seen up to the left from here.

Access

The crags in the Eglwyseg Valley lie on open ground owned in general by the Grosvenor Estates and leased out to local farms as open pasture for sheep grazing or as in the case of Craig y Forwen (Worlds End) to the Forestry Commission for a timber plantation.

At present there seems little opposition to the presence of climbers if the correct approach paths are used. This situation can obviously change if the correct procedures are abused or irritated by climbers taking short cuts.

The whole valley does come under the watchful eye of the Naturalist and RSPB Trusts who are answerable to the Grosvenor Estate. Both Trusts would ideally like the crags and screes to remain undisturbed by climbers so that the flora and fauna along with the bird life continue to thrive in as near a natural state as possible. The recent spate of enthusiasm for riding motor-cycles over the most undulating ground possible has brought the Trusts led by local farmers out in arms due to the death of several sheep and the crossing of valuable land. As yet any written or verbal restrictions have not been imposed on climbers. As lovers of the outdoors and all that it entails, climbers should appreciate fully the consequences of a violation of this common code of conduct, when on such a precious part of our countryside, if the sport is to continue independent of rules and regulations.

The birds and tiny alpine flowers which occasionally show their heads on the quieter cliffs, especially Craig Arthur and Monks Buttress are particularly rare to this part of the country. The nesting season does as always coincide with the start of the climbing season, when we are at our keenest, February to late June. It is in the interest of all who climb on the crags in this valley, that one uses some discretion during these months, especially if there are signs of nesting activity and to steer clear of a route, crag or situation which may disturb the nesting birds.

AS WITH ALL OTHER AREAS IN THIS GUIDEBOOK THE INCLUSION OF A CLIFF OR ROUTES UPON THEM **DOES NOT** MEAN THAT ANY MEMBER OF THE PUBLIC HAS THE RIGHT OF ACCESS TO THE CRAG OR THE RIGHT TO CLIMB UPON IT, THE ACCESS NOTES ARE A GUIDE NOT A PERMIT. IF IN DOUBT ASK FOR PERMISSION.

Character

The atmosphere generated in this valley varies considerably from crag to crag. On some a complete feeling of almost overwhelming exposure and seriousness only experienced on major crags, while on other more secluded crags, which reek of sweet smelling pines, there lies a relaxing calm atmosphere which all so often is the ingredient for limits to be pushed and standards raised.

The rock itself varies from excellent quality heavily cracked Carboniferous limestone with occasional shattered bands which are not, on any route, too loose to climb. The actual grain of the rock is very fine so friction is not put to great use as most of the climbing is on small face holds and pockets. Some routes appear to have short loose sections but unless mentioned in the route description most of the rock will be found to be solid and well cleaned. With more use, remaining pockets of mud and vegetation will disappear as many of the routes have not had second ascents.

The rock does have an advantageous tendency of drying out amazingly fast, even after heavy falls of rain and there is always a wind of some description to help the process.

Amazingly this perfect geological feature is not steeped in climbing history, as possibly it should be, yet many of the obvious lines had been climbed before 1970. Very few people, including myself after considerable investigation, know who made the first ascent of the early routes. In many ways I will regret the publication day of this guidebook as I have spent many days climbing in this valley alone or with a companion, never having to queue or listen to others shouting directions etc. and yet those mountains to the west have for too long enticed the climber past the treasures of this valley.

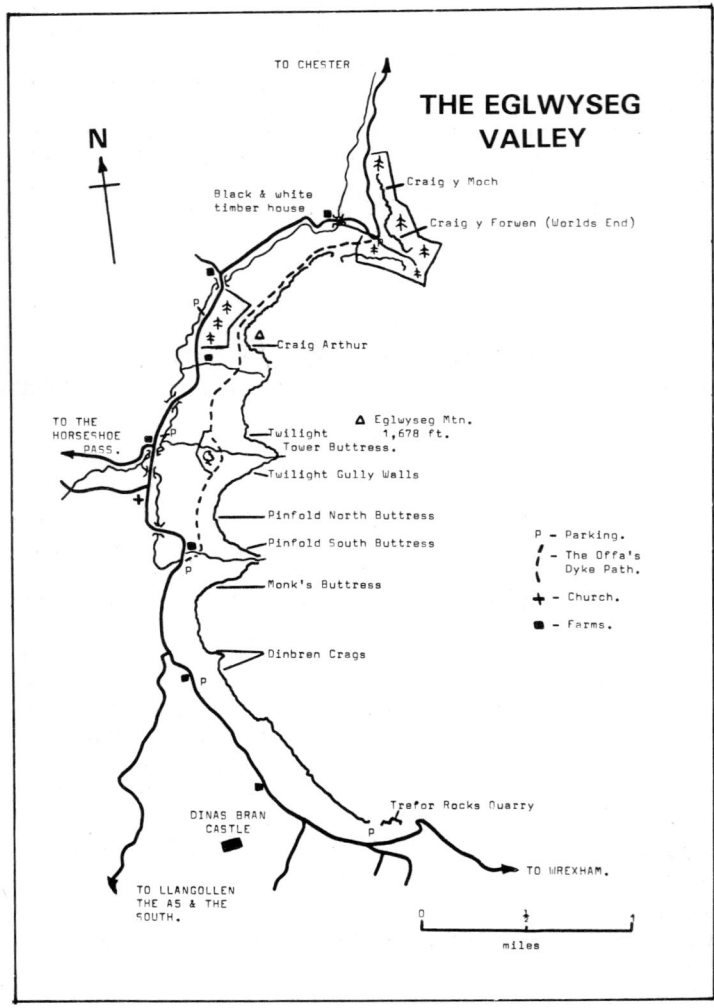

THE EGLWYSEG VALLEY

TO CHESTER

N

Craig y Moch

Black & white timber house

Craig y Forwen (Worlds End)

Craig Arthur

TO THE HORSESHOE PASS.

△ Eglwyseg Mtn.
1,678 ft.

Twilight Tower Buttress.

Twilight Gully Walls

Pinfold North Buttress

Pinfold South Buttress

Monk's Buttress

Dinbren Crags

P – Parking.
ʃ – The Offa's Dyke Path.
+ – Church.
■ – Farms.

DINAS BRAN CASTLE

Trefor Rocks Quarry

TO WREXHAM.

TO LLANGOLLEN THE A5 & THE SOUTH.

0   ½   1

miles

Camping

The official camp site for the Eglwyseg Valley is at Wylfa Farm MR. 213428. The Offas Path does follow the foot of the escarpment and many people camp on open spaces along this path, although these are usually just overnight stops. Camping is possible, but not official, on open land by the ford below the crags at Craig y Forwen (Worlds End), MR. 232479. There are no facilities at Worlds End for camping and already there are shameful signs of previous campers; litter, sawn down trees, damaged fences, etc., so please regard the land as your own and consider others and PLEASE TAKE ALL LITTER HOME WITH YOU OR IT WILL ONLY BE A MATTER OF TIME BEFORE RESTRICTIONS ARE IMPOSED.

CRAIG Y FORWEN (WORLDS END)

O.S. Ref. 234478.   O.S. Sheet No 117. 1:50,000

Situation

Craig y Forwen lies four miles north of Llangollen at the very head of the Eglwyseg River Valley, high above the small road and ford, guarded below by a steep scree. Tucked away in the narrow confines of this deeply cut valley amongst a pine forest the crag is only visible when almost at its base.

Parking and Approach

There is adequate parking at the ford below the crag or a hundred yards down the road on a larger open area of grass. The parking for this crag is also the first option for the approach to Craig Arthur.

Approach to the Upper Tier of the crag is by the obvious path beyond the ford and stile and up to where the valley narrows considerably and the Upper Tier drops to meet the path.

For climbs on the Middle and Lower Tiers approach by attacking the scree direct after passing over the stile.

Access

SEE THE MAIN ACCESS NOTES FOR THE EGLWYSEG VALLEY AS A WHOLE.

Character and Layout

This three tiered cliff at the head of this beautiful valley in a dominating, castle type position above the stepping-stones and ford, is in general composed of good solid Carboniferous Limestone. As with the rest of the escarpment down the valley there is an almost embarrassing plethora of cracks, corners and chimneys separated by steep and often overhanging walls with entertaining bulges and roofs.

Apart from Craig Arthur and the Pinfold Crags this collection of cliffs is probably the most impressive and certainly the most well used. On first encounters the Upper Tier block attracts one instantly to its steep walls and the fine collection of classic cracks, corners and grooves in a good position. On closer inspection one will quickly realise that each tier can display very individual tempting lines on good rock.

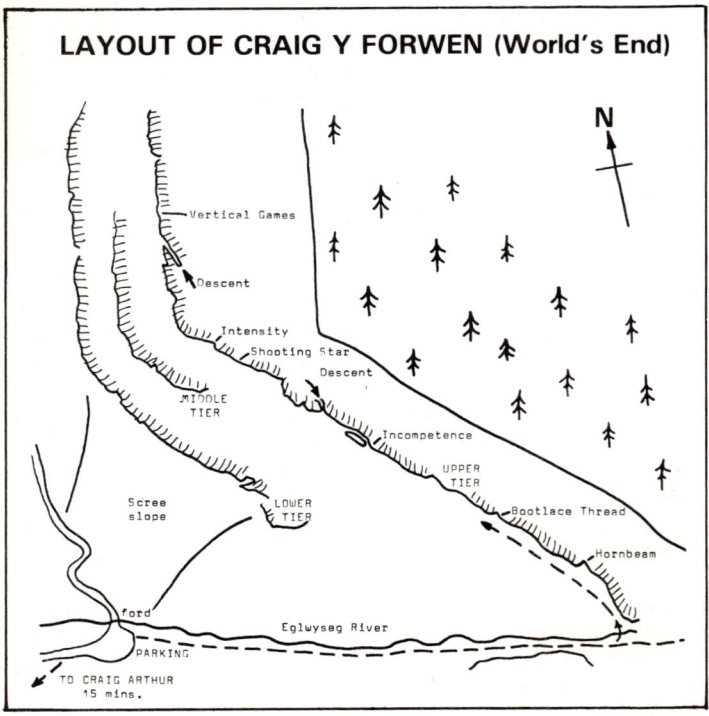

LAYOUT OF CRAIG Y FORWEN (World's End)

All three tiers are **NOT** prone to drainage problems and after even heavy rain the rock dries very quickly, with the crag facing south and lying at the head of the valley there is often a good drying wind. In winter the general aspect of the cliff often makes it an ideal choice even for a full day out and its proximity to the road makes it equally suitable for an evening's visit.

On some of the crags in this valley there are, unfortunately, small white squares painted at the foot of nearly all the older established routes, this practice took place several years ago and is most apparent at Craig y Forwen (Worlds End).

The Climbs

On all three tiers the routes are described from right to left as one is facing the rock.

The Upper Tier

1. RECESSSION BLUES   VS
    4b.   At the extreme right-hand end of The Upper Tier, close to where it meets the path, is an obvious flake crack with a small tree at 10ft. Start 10ft right of this and climb the small overhang, strenuous, below a crack, move left and up the easier blank wall to the top.

2. END FLAKE   HV Diff*
    The flake crack just right of the pine tree at 10ft, hard to start.

3. SHELFWAY   HV Diff
    Left of End Flake is a small pine tree at 10ft. Climb to the tree from a short corner and make a leftward rising traverse up large ledges.

4. COLTSFOOT CRACK   HVS*
    5a-.   15ft left of the start of Shelfway is a steep layback corner crack, follow this and the corner above to finish as for Shelfway.

    Some 15ft further left is a small flake corner ending in a ledge at 10ft, above the ledge is a flaky wall with a small overhang just above half height. The next three climbs start from the foot of the corner.

5. RIGHT EDGE   VS
    4a. Starting just right of the flake corner crack, climb the right edge of the flakes.

6. STRAIGHT EDGE   H Severe
    Starting at the corner crack climb almost straight up to the top.

7. LEFT EDGE   Severe
    Climb the corner crack and the left edge of the prominent flakes.

45

8. COLTSFOOT CORNER   Severe
    Climb the corner 10ft left of the edge climbs, either start direct
    or traverse in from the right.

The cliff now bulges into steep walls.

9. HORNBEAM   2
    6a. On the nose of the bulge is a steep short corner and line of
    weakness above, follow these with two peg runners in place.
    Hard.

10. HORNBLOWER   1
    5a + . Left of Hornbeam is a steep wall a fine crack from half
    height upwards. Climb to the crack and up starting at the white
    square.

11. HORNY   1
    5b. Start as for Hornblower at the white square. Climb up the
    right-ward trending flake crack and steep slab to join Horn-
    beam at half height. Move up rightwards to a steep broken
    crack close to the finish of Coltsfoot Corner. A good well
    protected route.

12. HORNWALL   1
    5b-. 25ft left of Hornbeam a small horizontal tree grows out of
    the wall. Climb direct to a small tree on the right of the
    horizontal tree and up the steep thin crack above.

13. HORNBEAM WALL   Mild VS
    4a. Climb to the horizontal tree and the broken wall above.

14. AS YEW LIKE IT   Severe
    Beyond the horizontal tree is an old Yew tree. Climb the wall to
    the tree and the broken crack above.

15. BOOTLACE THREAD   4**
    5c. Climb the obvious Twisting Corner for a few feet and using
    a good hold above a 'psychological bootlace thread' swing right
    onto the slab, move right and follow it with great difficulty to
    the top. A direct start can be made by climbing straight up to
    the slab. Bold climbing.

16. TWISTING CORNER   H Severe
    The steep corner to the top.

Continuing left a large open groove is reached with a white scar
left from a recent rockfall. On the right is a ragged crack and right
again is a flaky groove.

17. WHITE GROOVE   Severe
    Climb the flaky groove.

18. **WHITE CRACK** H Diff.
Climb the ragged crack. The wall on the right can also be climbed at Hard Severe.

19. **SCARFACE GROOVE** Diff.
The large open groove with care.

20. **GARDENER'S QUESTION TIME** Severe
20ft left of Scarface Groove is a small pinnacle with a recently fallen flake behind it. Climb the vegetated wall just right of the pinnacle.

21. **FLAKELESS GROOVE** H Severe
From the top of the fallen flake climb the groove trending left at the top. A slightly harder finish can be made to the right.

22. **BLACK PATH** HVS
5a. To the left of Flakeless Groove and high up on the bulging wall is a small tree, climb to this by a small bending groove. A steep route.

23. **ASHGROVE PRELIMS** VS*
4c. The obvious lay-back crack and groove following the shallow corner of cracks on the left at the top, 15ft left of the small tree on Black Path.

24. **CRACKSTONE RIB** HVS
5a. Climb Ashgrove Prelims for 10ft, traverse left onto the rib up into a scoop and the top.

25. **ASHGROVE** V Diff.
Up the deep flake crack to the large Ash tree and beyond.

26. **INSECURE** VS
4a. Around the corner left of Ashgrove is a zig-zag crack in the steep wall. Climb on up the large blocks and crack above.

27. **INCOMPETENCE** HV Diff.***
The deep crack left of Ashgrove and the pinnacle above. An excellent climb for its grade.

28. **INSPIRATION** H Severe*
Left of Incompetence on the wall is a fist sized crack which is climbed to the second flake on Inelegance and followed to the top.

29. **INELEGANCE** V Diff.**
Start by either crack to reach the top of the huge flake and up right over two remaining flakes to join Incompetence and gain the top.

The cliff bulges forbiddingly now until the descent gully is reached. The descent starts on steep grass and polished rock which requires care in damp conditions. Halfway down the descent it is possible to branch off down a cave-like chimney or continue down the gully to finish with an easy rock step, in both cases.

30.   **ROUGH CUT**   VS
      4a. 10ft right of the descent gully is a crack which is followed to a flake with a dead tree behind it. Finish either straight up or move right and finish over another flake.

31.   **SQUIRM**   Diff.
      Climb the main right-hand descent gully.

32.   **THE WORM**   H Severe
      On the face between the two descents are two crack leading to a groove and a dead tree near the top, climb this, the left-hand crack is slightly harder and requires a move right at half height to join the groove.

33.   **A'CHEVAL**   V Diff.
      The cave-like chimney used as an alternative descent.

34.   **FALL OUT**   HVS**
      5a. 10ft left of A'Cheval, climb the steep crack to finish in the trees. a typical steep limestone crack with excellent protection.

35.   **HELLS ARÊTE**   3.
      5c. The rounded arête left of Fall Out. Hard to start and poorly protected.

36.   **OPEN BOOK**   Severe
      Climb the open corner mainly by the right wall. A nice route.

37.   **SUICIDE CRACK**   3*
      5c + The left wall of the Open Book corner is climbed by a very technical and physically demanding thin crack.

38.   **BUTTER ARÊTE**   2**
      5b. Left of Suicide Crack is a rounded arête. Climb to a thin crack and good runner on the right of the arête, move onto the arête and follow it getting gradually harder to the top. Poorly protected.

39.   **IVY GROOVE**   VS
      4b. Climb the groove left of Butter Arête and just right of the large yew tree supported by a pedestal of rock.

    Behind the large yew tree is a deep chimney which provides an easy descent gully or a climb at Moderate.

40.   **WINDHOVER**   3***
      5c. Climb the shallow white mottled scoop left of the large yew

tree to below the severely overhanging short wall split by a finger crack. The scoop is hard to start and protect but the crack adds a superb finish. One of the best routes of its grade on the crag.

41. WINDY   HVS**
5a. The obvious crack which forks at 10ft. Follow the left fork which is just right of the blunt arête with a steep finish.

42. CLARTUM CORNER   Mild Severe
The right-hand of the twin cracks up to the lower of the two yew trees finishing on the rounded arête.

43. CLARTUM CRACK   Mild Severe
Climb either of the two left-hand cracks and the ill-defined corner up behind the yew trees.

From Clartum Crack the cliff continues as a steep wall with an undercut base almost to the left-hand skyline with few weaknesses.

44. FOSSIL FINISH   H Severe
Halfway along the wall above a small hole is a crack, climb this.

45. TRIPE & LANDAH   HVS
5a. Just left of Fossil Finish is a very direct crack line, this is climbed passing an old peg runner.

46. SHOOTING STAR   4***
6c. Fringing the blank wall left of Tripe and Landah is an obvious rightward trending overhang line up from the base of the wall. This line is followed up to a crack through the overhang where it changes direction, peg runner in place. The hardest route on the crag to date.

47. YEW & ME   HVS*
5b. Left of Shooting Star are two yew trees one above the other growing out of the wall. Climb the steep short wall to the lower tree, move left to climb the easier wall and thin crack to the top.

48. GOING BAD   3
5b. Left of Yew and Me the steep walls end with a short overhung corner and pillar of rock. Climb the corner and the left side of the pillar to continue up the crack which frizells out in the wall above, swing right to a good ledge hold near to the top, strenuous.

49. GONE BAD   1*
5b – . Climb the tiny groove on the right of the wild rose bushes following the crack to the broken overhang moving right below it to finish with an exposed layback up to the right.

50. **INTENSITY** HVS**
5a. Once the hardest route in the valley, strenuous but very well protected. Climb the deep overhanging crack left of the wild rose bushes.

51. **CLOSE TO THE EDGE** 2*
5b. Start as for Intensity. Climb the deep crack and traverse left across the steep slab below the overhang. Layback up around the roof by a thin finger crack to a good hold and up the easier groove to the top.

52. **CRAZNITCH CRACK** H Severe
The rightward leaning chimney crack is full of chockstones.

53. **ABANDONMENT** A1
Around the main bulging wall to the left of Craznitch Crack is a large blank wall. Climb the faint staggered crack up the centre of the wall with a few free moves to start and finish.

54. **WITHER** Diff.
The chimney full of huge boulders and chockstones.

55. **IVY CRACK** Severe
The fine deep crack with ivy growing at the top.

56. **SLITHER** VS
4c. Start as for Ivy Crack and climb the crack in the left wall to the dead tree at the top.

57. **XUXU** 1
5a. From the top of the large flake just left of the start of Ivy Crack pull over the bulge, strenuous, move left and finish up the wall to the right of the yew tree.

58. **HALF & HALF** Severe
The very obvious chimney to a chockstone at 20ft and up the right wall once inside the chimney.

59. **HEART OF DARKNESS** 3**
5c. Climb the superb rounded arête on the left of Half & Half in a far more serious position than one would expect considering its closeness to the chimney.

60. **TAERG WALL** 2***
5c. A first class route with a big crag atmosphere due to its position high above the ford, very photogenic. Start in the centre of the large wall left of Half & Half. Either climb a flake crack to a hand traverse line at 15ft moving left along this to a good crack and runners, or climb direct to the crack at the left-hand end of the hand traverse line by a steep faint crack. Move up to a good

ledge on the right and make a hard move up past a good peg runner to the top.

61. **LES ELEPHANTS** VS
4c. The slightly leaning chimney crack with chockstones. Hard to start.

62. **JENNIFER CRACK** H Severe**
4b. The obvious fine looking vee-groove.

63. **STING** H Severe*
4b. Left of Jennifer Crack is an ash tree on the arête near the top. Climb the large flake and the righ-hand crack passing the ash on its left.

64. **QUILL** Mild VS
4c. Climb the crack directly above the left side of the large flake at the foot of Sting.

Left of Quill is an obvious although slightly hidden descent gully when viewed from the wrong angle.

65. **DAGGA** Mild Severe
10ft left of the foot of the descent gully is a vegetated crack with a precariously perched block at 25ft, climb this crack to the block and the crack above.

66. **VERTICAL GAMES** 2***
6b. An exceptional piece of rock providing exceptional climbing with devious protection, a must. Start just left of the vegetated crack for Dagga at a steep crack. Climb the crack to horizontal break, move left to the short flake crack which fizzels out at 8ft in the smooth upper wall. Climb this crack to a good pocket a runner on the left, step up right and then back left with a very long reach to gain a good hold at the start of the leftward slanting continuation crack. With great difficulty crank up to a much higher good hold and then the top.

67. **DURBAN POISON** VS*
5a. Left of Vertical Games is a large ash tree growing out of the wall. Gain the undercut crack and climb to the tree, continue up the crack to the top.

68. **FINER FEELINGS** 1**
5b. A steep route with a strenuous start on good rock. From the top of a slightly leaning block climb the steep crack on the right of the large yew tree and the twin cracks above passing a small whitebeam tree on the left near the top.

The wall to the left of Finer Feelings has been climbed by a poor route which traverses in from the left to climb a steep crack in the wall at HVS 5a. Beyond this the walls become very loose and broken with no real routes worth mentioning.

The Middle Tier

The climbs are described from right to left, with the easiest means of descent down a narrow gully at the right end, all directions facing the rock. A large yew tree crowns the top of the right-hand end of the tier.

69. MARJOUN   HVS*
    5a. Below and right of the yew tree is a steep leaning crack. An arrow is marked on the rock. A difficult move is made to gain the upper left-hand crack.

70. MR. FLAY   H Severe
    The thin crack directly below the yew tree up the orange coloured slabby groove.

71. SLIM CHANCE   Mild VS
    4a. Follow the thin cracks 10ft left of Mr. Flay. Hard to start.

72. CAKE WALK   V Diff.
    Just right of the large embedded flake is a grass filled crack, follow this and the shorter crack leading to the Upper Tier.

73. HANDJAM   Severe
    On the left of the large embedded flake is a crack which widens above.

74. LAYBACK WITH ME   H Severe
    The obvious layback crack.

75. RUMBLE   Diff.
    15ft left of Handjam is a large crack containing jammed blocks, climb the crack.

To the left of this the tier merges with grass. Further on, the tier re-appears but there are few routes worthy of description.

The Lower Tier

Facing the rock, the routes are described from right to left with an easy descent at either end of the tier or just left of the centre.

76. OUJA CHIMNEY   Diff
    This is an obvious deep broken chimney just left of where the tier starts to break at its right-hand end.

77. THE NOSE   V Diff.
    The twin cracks on the left of Ouja Chimney.

78. **PICTURE ARÊTE** VS+ **
4c. Up the arête on its left between The Nose and Brown Cracks. Move left at half height to below a bulge and continue up the steep crack. A better route than it appears, with excellent potential for photographs.

79. **BROWN CRACKS** Severe
The twin cracks up some doubtful rock.

80. **GANJAH** Severe*
The groove 10ft left of the twin cracks of Brown Cracks.

81. **BLACKDOG** VS
4c+. A shallow groove containing a thin crack 6ft right of Black out.

82. **BLACK OUT** VS*
4c. Climb the black groove directly below the large bush. Small wires for protection and interesting steep climbing.

83. **LA DI DA** 2*
5b. Gain shallow white scoop which is capped by a small roof at 20ft. Finish straight over the roof. A good climb although poorly protected until the last moves.

84. **BRINKMAN** 2
5a+. The fine crack in the wall 15ft right of the obvious layback crack of Planerium. Strenuous with marginal protection, one peg in place.

85. **PLANERIUM** Severe***
The fine semi-layback crack up a square cut corner.

86. **CAVEMAN WALL** 2
5b. The walls left of Planerium now become very steep and slightly loose for a short distance. A small cave at 7ft is gained with good holds above to a ledge. The broken wall above to the top. Doubtful rock.

87. **ICICLE OF DEATH** 3**
5c. Thin rightward trending cracks lead up to a rectangular overhang at 20ft. Traverse left with increasing difficulty below small roofs to finish up an easy rake. A good route of character.

88. **MUSCLE BOUND** 2*
5b+. A thin crack climbs the wall 5ft right of the obvious layback crack of Plas Uchaf. A peg at 30ft provides little comfort on a technically hard route.

89. **PLASUCHAF CRACK** Severe**
The layback with a sapling at 12ft, a nice route.

90. THE CAUSE HVS
5a. A short steep crack up the wall below and to the right of the large yew tree.

One or two routes of an easy standard can be found up the broken rocks below and left of the large yew tree, but none are worth describing.

91. CATO Severe
An embodied flake just right of the holly bush. Step off the flake and traverse left to climb a groove and wall to the top.

92. HOLLY TREE WALL Severe
Climb the wall up to the holly tree trending in from the left of the cave, then the groove above.

The tier now breaks down for 100 yards to a point where an easy descent is possible down grass ledges. The wall reappears with very few lines long enough worth mentioning, but there are several interesting boulder problems. The first main feature is the groove and detached pillar of Pisa.

93. HYPERTENSION 4
5b +. Very sustained with almost no protection. 15ft right of the groove of Pisa is a vague depression trending up the wall to the right, this is followed.

94. PISA Severe
A groove above a yew tree with a right wall consists of a large detached pillar. Avoid the yew tree by the right wall, move left and carefully up the groove.

95. SUN SPOTS HVS
5a +. Climb the rounded nose which is covered with orange markings, on the right of the vegetated groove of grass. Move right at 20ft to climb a broken crack. A delicate, fingery start if done properly.

96. GRASS HV Diff.
The large groove full of grass, loose blocks and trees. A poor route!

97. DIAMOND VS + *
5a. Climb directly to the large diamond shaped overhang at 25ft, with a peg runner at halfway. Move left and follow the groove above, loose.

98. DIAMOND SOLITAIRE 2 **
5b. From the large diamond shaped roof on Diamond move up and right to a horizontal break which is followed to two small trees which mark an exit to the top. Exciting climbing, some-

times wet.

99. TREE   VS
4c. A steep short wall to the left-hand of two trees and shallow grooves to an exposed finish.

100. BUSH   Severe*
Some 60ft from the left end of the tier is a deep crack with a tree and boulder propped up against it at 20ft. A classic route for its grade.

CRAIG ARTHUR
O.S. Ref 224471   O.S. Sheet No. 117. 1:50,000

Situation
This very impressive cliff sits high up on the valley side in a dominating position near the head of the valley and facing due west. It is difficult to actually miss the crag when driving in either direction through the valley, although it is at its most impressive when viewed coming from the direction of Llangollen (south).

Parking and Approach
Parking for Craig Arthur is difficult and consideration for other passing vehicles and access for local land owners should be thought of when seeking a parking place along this narrow lane. There are only two official approaches, all others should be disregarded as they will undoubtedly cross restricted land.

1. Good parking with a long walk-in (15-20 mins.)
Parking by the ford at Worlds End MR.233478 walk a few yards downhill to a stile marking the start of a trail through the pine forest (Offas Dyke Pathway). Follow this trail until it exits from the forest after some five minutes. Continue to follow the contour level keeping below the escarpment until after some ten minutes the top corner of the large pine forest below Craig Arthur is reached. From here Craig Arthur is visible and a path has been constructed which leads up the scree to the northern end of the crag.

2. Difficult parking with a steep quick walk-in (10-15 mins.)
Parking is in one of the enlarged lay-by/passing places between the small river near Ty Canol Farm MR.222475 and the southern end of

56

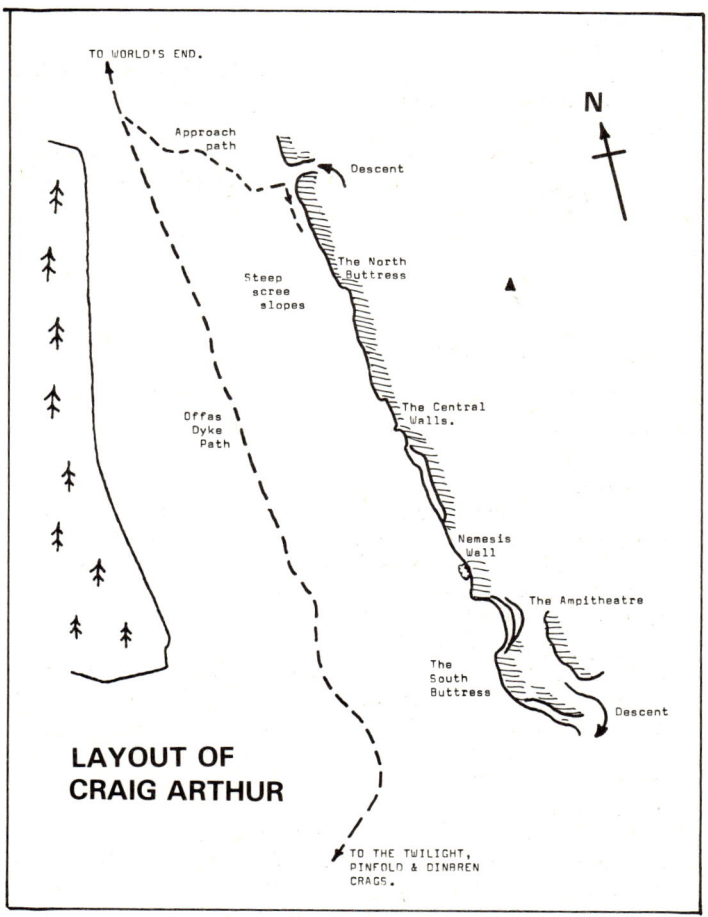

TO WORLD'S END.

Approach path

Descent

The North Buttress

Steep scree slopes

Offas Dyke Path

The Central Walls.

Nemesis Wall

The Ampitheatre

The South Buttress

Descent

N

LAYOUT OF CRAIG ARTHUR

TO THE TWILIGHT, PINFOLD & DINBREN CRAGS.

the pine forest MR.219470. A few yards south of the small river bridge at Ty Canol Farm is an old single gate, please keep it closed. Pass through this, follow the track up through a sheep pen and up the hillside northwards on the uphill side of a fence until the remains of a wall beside a wire fence stretching uphill is reached, follow this to the top of the field passing a huge boulder. Cross the fence and follow the path back right (south) to the edge of the pine forest.

From here Craig Arthur is visible and a path has been constructed which leads up the scree to the northern end of the crag.

PLEASE COMPLY CLOSELY TO THESE APPROACHES. AS YET NO RESTRICTIONS HAVE BEEN IMPOSED BUT OBVIOUSLY ABUSE WILL CREATE THEM!

DO NOT APPROACH THE CRAG DIRECT VIA THE WHITE COTTAGE 'TAN Y CRAIG' MR.220469.

ACCESS
IMPORTANT THAT ALL CLIMBERS READ THE ACCESS NOTES FOR THE EGLWYSEG VALLEY.

Character and Layout
This impressive crag extends horizontally for almost 1,200ft and vertically varying between 120ft and 150ft. Due to its westerly aspect a wind of some kind is almost always present, more often than not this can be an advantage to speedy drying sometimes a matter of minutes in summer, occasionally it can add considerable atmosphere to a route when it is blowing a gale. The sun is generally on the crag at the latest by midday onwards which makes this an appealing venue for not only full days here but a good summer evening choice.

Although there appears to be some loose sections of rock, many of the routes either skirt these areas or very little loose rock still remains. Pitons are in place on the routes for protection and should be left in place. On the girdle,, which is probably one of the best of its kind in the country, there are actually enough peg runners to hardly warrant taking any chocks on the route.

As with many other limestone cliffs all the routes, from the easiest to the most imposing, are very exposed. The height of the crag lies at 1,300ft and the very steep scree slope below this adds to the sometimes overwhelming feeling of exposure and vulnerability to the atmosphere which helps to enhance the superb quality of many of the climbs here. The steepness as always on limestone is very deceptive and Craig Arthur is no exception and should never really be underestimated.

The cliff is roughly split into four main sections. The North Buttress, Central Walls, Nemesis Wall and The South Buttress.

The left-hand end of the North Buttress is marked by an obvious detached pillar, Arthur's Pillar, which also marks the start of a line of varying sized overhangs continuing across the steep walls to the right for approximately 150ft, at half height. These large overhangs end at a steep crack up which Three Dimensions finds its way strenuously. The overhangs start again some thirty feet above, near to the top of the cliff, and continuing into a broken bay. Right of the bay, the overhangs diminish again on a rounded buttress which is split at half height by a superb crack with a steep slab at its base, taken by the equally superb Manikins of Horror. Right of this smooth buttress and wall, the overhang reappears in grand style high above a large yew tree. On the left of the overhang there is an impressive bottomless groove, Swalbr, and bounding its right side are the steep walls and blunt arête up which Tito and Digitron climb.

The angle now eases slightly for the Central Walls. The main features being the large horizontal waterworn bay at the foot of the cliff, overshadowed from above by a black wall and overhung block tower. Jungle Warfare takes the separated broken buttress right of the bay and the overhung tower, while Scary Fairy the exhilerating broken crack on its left and the sharp finger of flake above. A long vegetated terrace lies to the right and containing two large yew trees. Down to the right of the right-hand yew tree is a slabby wall which Charlain crosses and with a steep white groove on its right, Now and Then.

The walls now overhang alarmingly, streaked with black drainage marks on almost pure white rock, this is the Nemesis Wall. A sycamore tree provides ideal shade at the foot of the wall in summer. At the top of the wall is a large overhang and on the right an obvious square cut corner capped by an overhang. The Plop takes this corner swinging out right sensationally onto the right arête below the overhang. The left edge of the Nemesis Wall is perfectly divided from the Central Walls by a steep impressive crack which the highly technical and strenuous Survival of the Fastest follows. At the right-hand end the walls ease back and separate into a three tiered amphitheatre.

Almost a crag on its own the South Buttress is by no means a cliff of separate character. The obvious features here being the huge roof almost at the top of the cliff, and the obvious steep, smooth slab down to the left climbed by Double Crossbones.

The Climbs

All the routes are described from left to right (north to south) facing the cliff. The cliff at its extreme left-hand end, The North Buttress, dips rapidly into the rubble filled descent gully.

1.   ARTHUR'S PILLAR   120 feet Severe

Start 30ft right of the descent gully at a short corner.

Pitch 1. 90ft. 4b. Climb the short corner to the horizontal break,

move up and left to the base of the obvious detached pillar. Climb the pillar to exit left to gain a groove which is followed to a good belay ledge.

Pitch 2.   30ft. Move left and climb easily to the top.

2.   MONKEY'S CLAWS   120 feet E3
     Start as for Arthur's Pillar

Pitch 1.   80ft. 5b. Climb easily up rightwards over blocks and flakes to a large ledge at 60ft. Climb up to the overhang past an old peg and climb the overhang to a good hold on the right and a bush belay.

Pitch 2.   40ft. 5c. Move up right easily to below the steep bulging wall below some ivy. Traverse left with great difficulty to a good hold on the smooth wall, from this climb direct to the top by a thin flake crack. An unnerving pitch.

3.   THE FALL AND DECLINE   140 feet E3***
     Start at a broken corner directly below the obvious square-cut corner high up.

Pitch 1. 90ft. 5c + . Climb the steep wall past an old bent peg to the leftward trending flake crack, following this to the overhang. Move left to a hidden peg runner around the block to the left. Continue up the groove above for 10ft to step right onto the arête, peg belay on a small ledge. Not high in its technical grade but a classic, strenuous limestone pitch.

Pitch 2. 50ft. 5a. Climb up through the overhangs by an obvious break above the belay with an old peg runner. Thread belay on left at the top.

3A. LE CHACAL   120ft   E2***

An intimidating clas_sic, extremely strenuous although not highly technical. Start as for The Fall and Decline.

Pitch 1. 5c. Climb easily up to a prominent flake and up the steep wall following a thin crack past a poor peg runner as for The Fall and Decline, to a resting ledge at the foot of the steep left-ward trending crack, which that route takes. Move up the crack a few feet until it is possible, using a good hold on the steep

61

wall, to move into the obvious square cut corner, continue up this to the roof. Swing right on a fine exposed position to a peg runner in the horizontal break, using a good hold on the right gain this and climb the yellow wall above to good holds. Traverse right to a ledge and a bolt and peg belay.

Pitch 2. 5a. Move right and up into the steep flake crack which is followed to a whitebeam tree on the left, pass below this and then back right above it into an easy groove on the right which is followed to the top.

4. A TOUCH OF CLASS   215 feet E2***

Start as for The Fall and Decline. A superb route with excellent protection.

Pitch 1. 90ft. 5b. Climb easily to a ledge at 15ft on a horizontal break. Move to the right-hand end of the break and climb the steep wall to a good peg runner at the left end of the blank wall. Traverse right across the wall passing a peg to a hidden slab, moving up this to the roof and a peg belay.

Pitch 2. 60ft. 5a. Traverse right along the horizontal break to below the steep bottomless groove. Climb the groove to pass a thread and move right onto the shattered arête when level with a peg runner. Tree belay above, in the bay below a large overhang.

Pitch 3. 65ft. 4c. Move left across the steep wall to a good ledge on the rounded arête and up the wall to the top. A bold pitch for its grade.

Le Chacal, 1st ascent. Climber, Stuart Cathcart

5.   **THREE DIMENSIONS**   150 feet E2***
Start at a short corner beneath the right-hand end of the thorn
shrubs at 15ft in the horizontal break. Excellent climbing on
good rock.

Pitch 1.   85ft. 5b + . Climb to the right of the thorn shrubs moving
up to the prominent leftward pointing flake overhang, climb
this to a poor resting ledge and peg runner. Move right with
difficulty into the main crack and up to the large roof and
another peg. Step left and up into the bottomless groove
passing a thread, in place, moving right onto the shattered arête
when level with a peg above. Tree belay well back in the bay.

Pitch 2.   65ft. 5b. Move up into the corner on the left of the tree
and a good runner below the overhang pulling out over the roof
on slightly loose but good holds.

6.   **LEGACY**   140 feet HVS
Start at the left of a yew tree near to the base of the cliff below a
slab.

Pitch 1.   85ft 5a. Climb to an old peg at the foot of the smooth
slab at 30ft. Move down left slightly to a small ledge and
continue up diagonally leftwards over some loose rock to a tree
belay in a large bay.

Pitch 2.   70ft. 4b. Move right along the horizontal fault to the
rightside of the bay and climb the obvious slightly loose break.
Belay well back.

7.   **STRATEGEM**   130 feet E2*
Start as for Legacy below the obvious smooth slab at 30ft.

Pitch 1.   130ft. 5b. Climb to the old peg at the foot of the smooth
slab. Climb the slab to the bulge at the top, peg runner, and
climb the bulge out leftwards to a good runner in the horizontal
break (hard). Step right and continue to a small tree and large
blocks, following a stepped crack to the top. Belay on a buried
wire anchor well back.

8.   **MANIKINS OF HORROR**   130 feet E2***
On the right of the yew tree below the smooth slab of Stratagem
is a small cave, start on the right of this. A highly recommendable route.

Pitch 1.   130ft. 5c. Gain the horizontal break above the cave,
move left to a small corner and up to a peg runner. Delicate
climbing leads up around the blunt arête to the left onto the
smooth slab to the foot of the steep crack, peg runner. Climb
the steep crack passing three good pegs to a collection of pegs as

for the girdle. Move left and straight up passing a small tree to the top. Belay on a buried wire well back.

9. **SWLABR LINK**   140 feet **E3****
    Start as for Manikins of Horror. A desperate first pitch, superb highly technical fingery climbing, with good protection.

Pitch 1. 80ft. 6a + . Follow Manikins of Horror to the first peg above a small corner. Move up with increasing difficulty to a finger hole and passing another peg to the horizontal break. It is possible to by-pass the hard part by climbing Manikin of Horror and traversing in along the horizontal break. Follow the break right past two pegs and up an easier crack at its end to a large ledge and tree belay.

Pitch 2. 60ft. 5a. As for Swalbr pitch 2.

10. **SWLABR**   140 feet **VS****
    The original classic line of the crag, with a very good top pitch.

Pitch 1. 80ft. 4a. Climb up behind the left side of the large yew tree and move up the wall for a few feet. Traverse left into a broken groove and up to a large ledge and tree, belay below the left end of the large roof.

Pitch 2. 60ft. 5a. Climb the steep crack and bottomless groove above the left end of the ledge and tree belay. Belay well back on the buried wire anchor. Excellent protection and an airy pitch for its grade.

The main overhang right of Swlabr has been climbed directly above the large yew tree following a faint crack at A3.

11. **TITO**   145 feet **E1**
    Right of the large yew tree is a clean cut corner with a steep left wall and a slabby right wall.

Pitch 1. 70ft. 5b. Climb up into the corner and move out across the steepening slab passing a peg runner to a bulge and a good peg. Make a difficult move up and then traverse right a short way to gain a good thread belay below bulging overhangs.

Pitch 2. 75ft. 5a. The crack on the left of the thread is followed to a small tree. Move up easily, dubious rock, onto an orange lichen covered scoop and the top. A lonely pitch although not particularly hard.

12. **DIGITRON**   150 feet **E2*****
    80 feet right of the large yew tree is a steep rounded arête, with a small whitebeam tree on the left of the arête at 25ft. A sustained route.

Pitch 1. 90ft. 5b. Climb the steep wall to a peg runner at 10ft moving right to a shattered ledge up to a small whitebeam tree at the foot of a short corner. Climb the corner, peg runner, to a slab on the left. Follow a steep crack above, poor peg, to the overhang passing it on the right to gain the arête. Traverse right along a footledge around the arête to the yew tree and a belay in it.

Pitch 2. 60ft. 5c. Fight up out of the yew tree to the left and a horizontal crack, a peg and Karabiner. Move left to a good ledge on the arête. Climb the bulge above to the foot of an immaculate steep slab and a short crack with a good peg runner. Climb the crack to its top making a long reach up right to gain a good hidden pocket, and up to the small tree above and the top. An excellent pitch.

13. BADGE   130 feet E1
Right of Digitron near to the base of the cliff, are a number of overhangs below a steep blank wall. Start at the foot of the broken groove on the right of these overhangs.

Pitch 1. 80ft. 5c. Climb the small overhang, peg runner, into the groove following this past another peg moving right and then back left to belay in the large scoop. The difficult climbing is short lived and well protected at the start.

Pitch 2. 50ft. 4c. Move up the scoop behind the belay until blocked by the bulge, escaping out left across the steep wall with surprising ease using a large hold on the arête.

14. SCARY FAIRY   160 feet E2**
Start below the steep corner at the left end of the obvious smooth horizontal water worn bay. A good route with an airy top pitch.

Pitch 1. 80ft. 5c. Climb up around the bay into the steep crack by a strenuous swinging move and climb it to a good ledge on the left below the huge roof.

Pitch2. 80ft. 5b. Move to the left end of the ledge and climb up into the prominent V-groove, moving up it a few feet make a sensational swing left onto the arête of the groove and then up the yellow wall to the top.

15. JUNGLE WARFARE   120 feet HVS
Start at the foot of the deceptively easy looking broken scoop in the small separate pillar at the left end of the vegetated terrace and below the left-hand yew tree.

Pitch 1. 70ft. 5a. Climb the scoop by a large flake crack with a steep finish onto the steep grass terrace. Belay behind the large yew tree.

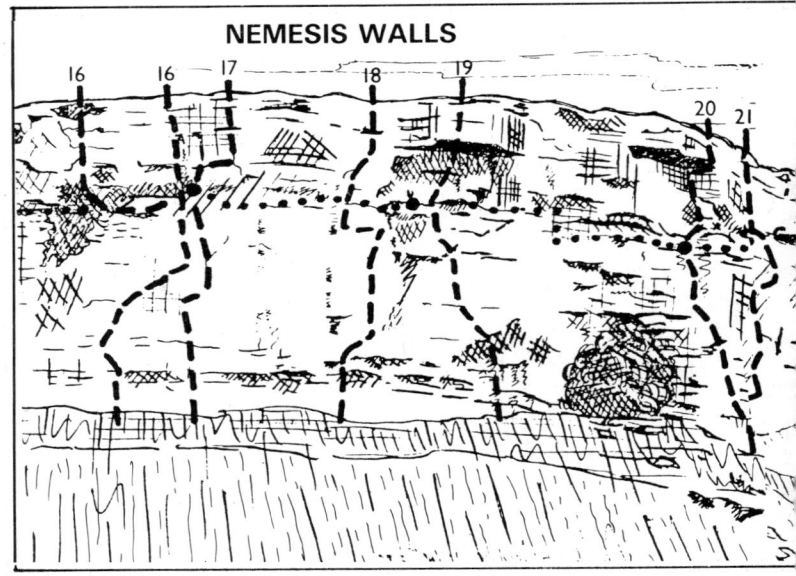

NEMESIS WALLS

Pitch 2. 50ft. 5a. Climb the yew tree and using a good hold step onto the wall, good runner on the right, moving left to a large block round:ng this to a small ledge. Ascend the steep yellow groove and cracks to the top.

16. CHARLAIN   120 feet HVS**

Below the right end of the grass terrace is a slabby wall. Start in the centre of the wall 10ft left of the foot of the white groove of Now and Then. An enjoyable route.

Pitch 1. 80ft. 5a. Climb easily to a horizontal break at 15ft and move up to a good peg runner with sling. Surmount the bulge and trend up right with increasing difficulty to another peg passing to gain the top of a large block. Step right up a short wall then left to a small ledge and tree belay.

Pitch 2. 40ft. 4b. Either climb the corner containing a tree behind the belay or better move left along the grass terrace for 20ft to climb the broken cracks to the top. Belay on the large boulder well back.

17. NOW AND THEN   140 feet E1*

Start at the foot of the steep white stained groove right of Charlain. The protection is spaced but very good with steep

CRAIG ARTHUR   SOUTH BUTTRESS

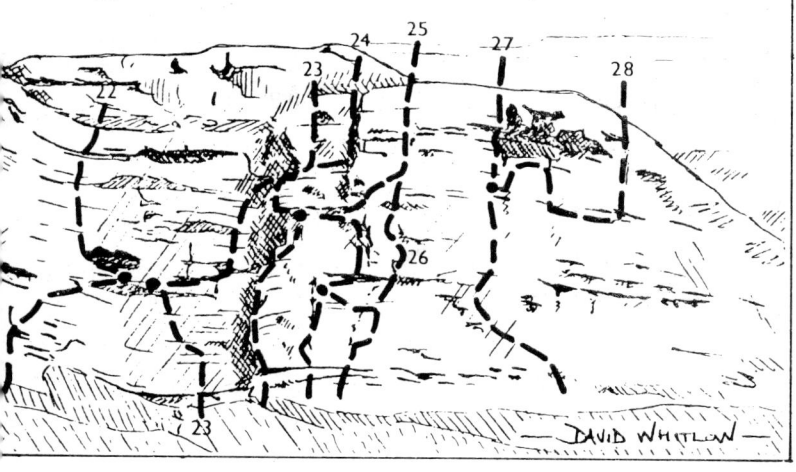

— DAVID WHITLOW —

technical climbing.

Pitch 1.   80ft. 5b. Gain the steep groove, peg runner, move up with increasing difficulty to another peg. Continue up and step right to a sloping ledge using side pulls with a good peg runner above the bulge on the left. Finish up a short broken wall to a small ledge and tree belay.

Pitch 2.   60ft. 5a. Move up and right to a whitebeam tree in the horizontal break, traverse out right for 10ft across the steep wall and up the wall and crack above to the top. Belay on the large boulder.

18.   SURVIVAL OF THE FASTEST   130 feet E4****
Probably the best and certainly one of the hardest routes in the area of exceptional quality throughout.
Start below the very steep crack at the left side of the Nemesis Wall.

Pitch 1.   130ft. 6b. Climb to a ledge above the overhang and below a diagonal crack containing some ivy. Move right into the main crack line, peg runner, and up to a good resting hold. Above are two good peg runners which are passed with great difficulty to another peg and a good undercut above. A bolt runner can be reached above the undercut, from here a long reach is made to a ledge on the left for a superb swing across the wall and up to a peg runner in the horizontal break. Pull onto the slab above which is followed to an easier crack leading to the top. Belay on the nearest large boulder.

The cliff now overhangs gently from top to bottom capped at the top by large overhangs. Two artificial routes climb this white wall only one however, is worth mentioning.

19. **NEMESIS**   130 feet A3
Start 30ft left of the large tree. (15 pegs with 3 poor bolts in place).
Pitch 1. 60ft. Up the bulge-like riblet and after 25ft move right into a scoop and exit left via a bolt into the obvious crack. Up the crack to a small roof which is surmounted with a long reach and climb into the groove above exiting left on bolts to a stance in etriers at the horizontal break.
Pitch 2. 70ft. Move left from the belay and up via a free move to a rising traverse line on the left. At the end of the traverse step into the prominent vertical corner, up this and over the 5ft roof until free moves above the lip lead to a stance just below the top.

20. **THE BIG PLOP**   120 feet E2 (1pt of aid)
20ft right of the large tree below a short wall.
Pitch 1. 70ft. 5b. Climb the short wall to a tree and continue up left following an easy broken crack past two more trees to a ledge. Climb the steep wall above the top tree, peg runner, to a small ledge left of a small bush, peg belay.
Pitch 2. 5ft. 6a. With one peg for aid, in place, move up into the steep corner, with difficulty pass another peg for protection and continue up the corner to make a swing right below the roof onto the arête and easier ground to the top. A highly demanding pitch in many ways.

21. **THE HOAX**   120 feet HVS
Start as for the Big Plop below the short wall and tree.
Pitch 1. 120ft. 5a. Climb the short wall to the tree at 8ft, move up right to the main crack containing the ash tree, peg on the left. Climb the crack above the tree moving right near the top to avoid loose rock before gaining the terrace. Pull up left from the terrace to the old wizzened yew tree to finish up right of the tree. Ground level impressions of the route will definitely deceive as the title denotes.

Right of The Hoax the walls merge into a three tiered amphitheatre with the height of the tiers diminishing in size towards the top.

22. **COLD FINGER** 130 feet HVS−

Start 20ft right of The Hoax at the foot of the rightward slanting slab.

Pitch 1. 75ft. 5a. Up onto the slab and follow it rightwards to the small overhangs, move right below these until the grass terrace can be gained. Tree belay on the right.

Pitch 2. 55ft. 4b. Move back left and climb out of the terrace by a shattered wall, continue easily to the top.

23. **OCTOPUS** 120 feet VS

Start directly below the tree on the terrace at a shattered wall.

Pitch 1. 65ft. 4c. Climb the broken wall to the tree on the terrace passing an old peg at 10ft.

Pitch 2. 55ft. 4c. Move right and climb the broken walls to the top terrace, move right along this to a tree and climb the easy wall fighting with a machete in hand through the bushes to the top. A poor route.

The Amphitheatre now emerges once again into steep walls, The South Buttress.

24. **SCRAPYARD THING** 130 feet HVS*

Just left of the obvious steep blank slab at the base of the left-hand side of the buttress is a large flaked crack facing left and above the overhang. A much better route than it appears.

Pitch 1. 80ft. 5a. Climb the overhang to gain the foot of the flake crack and climb this on its left for 20ft to stand on top of the detached flake which it forms. Make a delicate move up the wall to a peg runner and good hold, continue up rightwards to a small tree across the slab. Peg belay below the overhangs.

Pitch 2. 50ft. 5a+. Move left to climb the overhang with two peg runners onto the terrace. Walk right and up the obvious chimney groove to the top.

25. **DOUBLE CROSSBONES** 170 feet E3**

At the foot of the obvious steep blank rightward slanting slab below three overlaps. A technical line to start with an excellent top pitch.

Pitch 1. 70ft. 5c. Gain the foot of the steep slab and move up to a peg runner, climb the slab to the overhang and move left to a good ledge. Traverse left below the overhang for 20ft to a peg belay.

Pitch 2. 40ft. 5a. Climb the overhang on the right into the crack and corner which is followed to a good ledge and peg belay on the left as for Scrapyard Thing.

Pitch 3. 60ft. 5a. Move back right and gain the pointed prow below the large overhang, peg runner, move up right around the overhang, exposed, to the obvious traverse line. Traverse right to the break in the overhang above which is followed to the top.

DIRECT START   60 feet E3***
5c + . Climb almost directly to the first belay below the overhang via a horizontally cracked wall and a smooth shallow scoop with a poor peg. Excellent rock and highly technical climbing.

26.   SCOUSERS   150 feet E3 & A2
Start as for Double Crossbones at the steep slanting slab.

Pitch 1.   100ft. 5c & A2 Gain the foot of the slab and move up to a peg runner, climb the slab to the overhang and move left to a good ledge. Climb up right to a ledge below the steep walls and make a hard move to a peg which is used to gain a bolt ladder which leads to a ledge and belay.

Pitch 2.   50ft. 5a. Move left and up the break in the overhang to the top.

27.   GATES OF THE GOLDEN DAWN   150 feet E3***
Start on the centre of the South Buttress below the main overhang at the top and on the grass terrace at a point to the right of the yellow lichen scar. A fierce and exposed piece of climbing.

Pitch 1.   90ft. 5b. Gain the short steep groove left of the arched wall, make a difficult move up to a good hold on the left. Move up to a peg runner stepping right and up some dubious rock past a poor peg to a poor belay.

Pitch 2.   60ft. 6a. Climb up to the steep overhang above the belay passing a peg on the wall. Using a peg for aid climb the overhang to a good hold on the right which is passed with considerable difficulty to the top.

28.   THE DEADLY TRAP   180 feet E4
Start as for Gates of the Golden Dawn. A devious route requiring thought in rope positioning on the second pitch. A serious route.

Pitch 1.   90ft. 5b. As for the first pitch of Gates of the Golden Dawn.

Pitch 2.   90ft. 5c. Climb to a peg in the wall above the belay, move right into a short groove which is descended to a poor

   Gates of the Golden Dawn. Climber Stuart Cathcart. ▷
   The route climbs the thin crack in the roof above the climber.

footledge, traverse right along this at varying heights past a tree and climb a steep wall into a large flaked crack, passing three peg runners on the wall.

CRAIG ARTHUR GIRDLE 830 feet E2**** (pegs used for aid makes it VS).

Start as for Arthur's Pillar at the extreme left-hand end (northern) of the crag at a short corner 30ft right of the descent gully.

Pitch 1. 100ft. 4a. Climb to the precariously detached pillar, move up on the left of this groove. At the top of the groove traverse right to above the overhang and up a short corner on the right to the first peg belay.

Pitch 2. 100ft. 4b. Traverse right and drop down to the bedding plane below, peg runner. Continue right into an undercut niche, peg runner, and exit awkwardly right to traverse 20ft into a large bay and tree belay.

Pitch 3. 80ft. 3c. Climb across the back of the bay and drop down 10ft to reach an obvious terrace traverse line, peg runner. Follow the traverse line for 30ft and climb up to a small tree by a detached block, peg belay.

Pitch 4. 40ft. 5c. Move down for 15ft to a collection of pegs, traverse right with difficulty to a bay into this and so to a large ledge and tree belay. The original route took a line across the wall from the belay to a peg and thread which was used to lower ones self into the bay and so to the same tree belay.

Pitch 5. 100ft. 5b. Climb across to the right edge of the large bay and attain two bedding planes, peg runner, move up past two more pegs to some small trees. Follow the bedding plane rightwards until further progress is impossible, above is a small ramp capped by an overhang, move right from a peg runner below the overhang and down into the yew tree, move down to a tree belay.

Pitch 6. 60ft. 5b. Move right across the wall to a thin bedding plane and climb into a small corner, continue across an immaculate steep slab, two peg runners, and around the arête to a small ledge. Peg belay on right.

Pitch 7. 100ft. 5a. Climb right past a peg to a large ledge, from this move down slightly from a peg and across the steep wall to a yew tree. Pass behind the yew tree and continue to the next large yew tree halfway along the terrace.

Pitch 8. 100ft. 5b. Traverse the wall at the junction of rock and grass and drop down to an ash tree, the grassy broken wall on the right is crossed to a good ledge and peg runner. Swing down right and hand traverse into a scoop passing three pegs and exit around the steep arête to a small tree belay. A good pitch.

Pitch 9.   75ft. 5a. Move easily for 8ft and drop down to a peg runner into the final groove of Nemesis, continue to the bolts on Nemesis and into a small niche with an old wooden wedge for protection. Move down using a good hidden hold below the overhang to a very loose flake, possibly disappeared, and follow the obvious line right to a good stance around the arête. An airy pitch with some awkward moves but very photogenic.

Pitch 10.   80ft. 5a. Swing right past a small thorn bush and gain a ledge, peg runner. Move right to a peg at foot level and traverse right on good holds to the terrace. Climb the shattered wall on the left to the wizened yew tree and the crack on the right to finish.

A magnificent expedition with continuous good climbing.

THE TWILIGHT CRAGS

1.   TWILIGHT TOWER BUTTRESS
O.S.Ref. 223463   O.S. Sheet No. 117
2.   TWILIGHT GULLY WALLS
O.S. Ref. 224461   O.S. Sheet No. 117

Situation

These two small interesting buttreses can be found in the vicinity of the second tributary valley down from the ford at World's End. The most prominent buttress is the Twilight Tower Buttress which is easily inspected from the road junction at Plas yn Eglwyseg (MR.216462), high up on the left skyline of the deeply cut wooded tributary valley. The Gully Walls can be seen from the road junction stretching out rightwards (south) from the very head of the valley above the wood, but they are not really fully open to the road.

Parking and Approach

Parking on the grass verge on the north side of the road junction at Plas yn Eglwyseg (MR.214642), cross the hump backed bridge pass through the gate marked 'footpath' and follow the line of the stream on its right bank up to the woods at the top of the field. Continue up through the woods to the top tree line where a low fence is crossed and a faint path leads up the valley following the right bank of the stream until it disappears at a steep scree slope directly below the left-hand end of the Twilight Gully Walls. From here the Twilight Tower Buttress is easily reached by a steep path along the base of the broken tier running leftwards (north) out of the gully confines to the skyline where the crag is situated.

Access
SEE THE ACCESS NOTES FOR THE EGLWYSEG VALLEY AS A WHOLE.

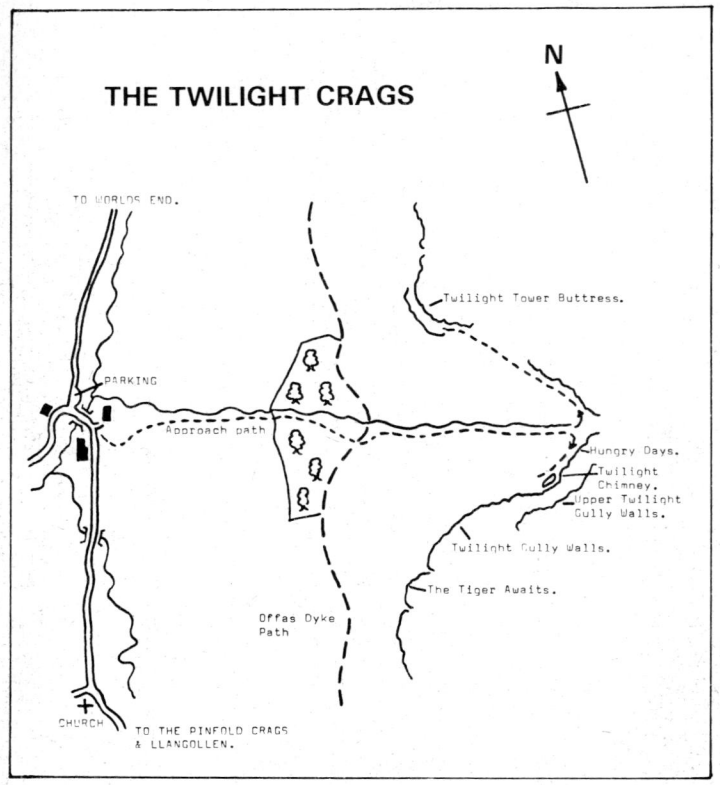

THE TWILIGHT CRAGS

N

TO WORLDS END.

Twilight Tower Buttress.

PARKING

Approach path

Hungry Days.
Twilight Chimney.
Upper Twilight Gully Walls.

Twilight Gully Walls.

The Tiger Awaits.

Offas Dyke Path

CHURCH
TO THE PINFOLD CRAGS & LLANGOLLEN.

Go-a-Go-Go, Twilight Tower Buttress ▷
Climber Dave Barker

Character and Layout

The climbs described are similar in length to those found on the many other crags in the valley, except for Craig Arthur, but on the Tower Buttress one is exposed completely to the elements and a certain amount of grand exposure being set high above the valley floor. The Gully Walls however, can be a little depressing on overcast days and even cause the mind to play tricks during twilight, but its north facing walls dry very quickly and stay cool on hot evenings thanks to an uncanny breeze which seems to blow constantly up the valley.

The rock found on the Twilight Tower Buttress is some of the best in the valley and naturally there are some of the best routes although these are limited due to it only being a small crag. The Twilight Gully Walls has over forty routes many of a high technical quality but unfortunately on a very dark rock which occasionally is loose especially on the very tops where there can often be large hanging scree slopes.

TWILIGHT TOWER BUTTRESS
O.S. Ref. 223463   O.S. Sheet No. 117 1:50,000

Layout

This small compact buttress forms the left promontory of this deep tributary valley.

There are two tiers to its make-up although the lower tier is rarely visited. The main upper tier sports an exciting central wall with a deep open chimney on its right capped by a large roof, which the excitingly wild High Impedance takes and where the equally bold Go A Go Go swings out of to ascend the steep main wall. To the left of this central wall the tier is broken by steep narrow walls, an excellent slabby wall marked with uncharacteristic pockets and cracks up which Sunday Driver climbs, and fine corners and arêtes with the finest corner of all, Funeral Corner, bordering the left-hand end of the tier. Left of the central wall the climbs are generally in the upper grades, but to the right there is a large selection of much easier grade routes following deep chimneys and cracks with Moncrieff taking the main challenge of the ivy-covered tower on its left.

All directions are given to mean when one is facing the rock with the routes being described from right to left (south to north) on both tiers, the upper tier is described first. During the approach to the upper tier the path traverses below the tier where it is short and broken until a short deep rightward facing descent chimney is reached with an obvious layback crack on its left, this is Sloth. It is possible to descend down behind the ivy covered tower on the right of the central wall, Ivy Tower Chimney, or at the left-hand end of the tier down one of several steep vegetated gullies.

The Climbs
The Upper Tier

1. **SLOTH** — V Diff
   At the right-hand end of the tier on the left of the descent chimney below an obvious layback crack. Climb the layback.

2. **FLAWSE** — V Diff
   Left of Sloth are loose cracks up the front of the buttress which are followed with some care.

3. **PREJUDICE** — Diff
   The pleasant chimney crack on the left of the buttress.

4. **PRIDE** — V Diff
   The cracked groove left of Prejudice.

5. **SIMIAN** — Diff
   The vegetated and tree choked wide crack.

6. **TO CUT A LONG STORY SHORT** — Mild VS
   4c. An enjoyable short climb with few runners. Climb the obvious small clean corner right of a yew tree.

7. **ONEGIN** — Severe
   The first crack left of the yew tree.

The face between To Cut A Long Story Short and Onegin has been climbed at about Severe but it is not particularly worthwhile.

8. **HELME'S HIGHWAY** — Mild Severe
   Left of Onegin is a shallow corner which is climbed with a difficult mid-section.

9. **THE CLEAROUT** — Mild VS
   4b. 6ft of Helm's Highway is a steep crack.

10. **SKULLION** — Mild VS*
    4b. Start at a large flake right of a tree and follow the thin cracks trending up slightly rightwards. An interesting route.

11. **COW PARSLEY** — V Diff
    To the left of Skullion is the ivy covered tower with a tree on its right which obscures the foot of two chimneys. Climb up past the tree and up the right-hand chimney.

12.   IVY TOWER CHIMNEY   V Diff
Climb past the tree and up the left-hand chimney.

13.   MONCRIEFF   V Diff
On the left of the ivy covered tower is a wide crack which is
climbed past a dead tree.

14.   ATTENUATION   VS*
4c. On the left of the start of Moncrieff is a narrow wall with
the obvious deep chimney and cave of High Impedance on its
left. Climb the narrow wall and up the short smooth slab and
groove with a difficult start. A worthwhile climb.

15.   HIGH IMPEDANCE   1**
A wild roof climb with excellent protection.
5b +. Climb up into the deep chimney and up to the cave.
Move up to a good thread and climb the roof crack direct with a
difficult finish into a short groove.

16.   GO-A-GO-GO   2***
5b. A bold exhilerating route. Climb as for High Impedance to
the cave below the large roof. Move out to the lip of the roof,
then swing left onto the steep main wall into an excellent flake
crack which is followed up and left to the top.

17.   WOODPIGEON CRACK   H Severe
4a. On the left side of the steep central wall is an elder tree.
Climb up left of the elder tree, then move back right to gain the
bird-scratched crack above.

18.   SUNDAY DRIVER   VS*
4c. An easy route to escape from but a fine climb on excellent
rock if followed throughout. Around the bulging arête to the
left of Woodpigeon crack is a slabby wall with a line of thin
cracks and pockets which are followed to a tiny ash tree where
the angle changes.

19.   LORAN   Severe
The crack past a small yew tree and the thin crack above or the
slab on the left to the top.

20.   RUTH'S RAMBLE   V Diff.
The next crack to the left of Loran past two dead trees with an
easier groove above.

21.   SIDESTEP   VS
4c. 10ft left of Ruth's Ramble below a steep wall and thin crack
immediately right of the start of Penetration Factor. Climb the
crack to a good handhold where the wall steepens, move right
to the edge and climb the groove just left of Ruth's Ramble.

22. **PENETRATION FACTOR** VS**
4c. The prominent widening crack on the left of the steep wall. A fine airy climb.

23. **INTER-DIGITAL PAUSE** HVS*
5a. Left of Penetration Factor is a rounded arête with the very obvious clean-cut corner of Funeral Corner on its left. Climb a line of thin cracks starting a few feet right of Funeral Corner, strenuous, past an old peg near the top. A difficult start with hidden holds.

24. **FUNERAL CORNER** H Severe***
4a. A classic. The fine clean-cut corner with a small roof near the top.

25. **EXTENSION** Mild VS
4b. Climb the arête on the left of Funeral Corner with a long reach at half-height.

26. **ON-LINE** Severe
A steep layback start leading to an easier groove above marks the leftmost extremity of the climbing on this tier.

The Lower Tier

27. **TERMINAL** VS
4c. Near to the right-hand end of the lower walls is a blunt rib with a deep groove on its left and a large chockstone near the top. Follow the thin cracks just left of the rib.

28. **OPEN TO OFFA'S** V Diff.
The deep groove with the large chockstone near to the top.

29. **RIBOFLAVIN** Severe
Just left of Open To Offa's is a sharp rib which is climbed passing a yew tree near to the top.

30. **INTERFACE** Mild VS*
4b. Left of Riboflavin is a large pinnacle with a crack up its face. A deep gully bounds the pinnacle on the right, climb the wall right of this.

31. **PINNACLE CRACK** HV Diff*
Climb the crack in the face of the pinnacle to its summit. From the top of this route one is positioned on the terrace directly below the excellent Penetration Factor on the upper tier which combined with Pinnacle Crack produces a fine climb.

TWILIGHT GULLY WALLS

O.S. Ref. 224461   O.S. Sheet No. 117. 1:50,000

Layout

Although the apparent long walk-in and the univiting colour of the rock may deter some climbers, those who do sample its true delights will realise its value, - steep interesting climbing on generally good rock.

There is only one tier with routes described on it, although there is a smaller tier set 100ft back from the top of the main tier which has some of the best bouldering in the area on it and is noted under a separate heading in the guide 'Bouldering'

The climbs are described from left to right starting at the very steep bulging walls with scattered overhangs at the head of the valley stream. Approximately 150ft right of the start of the tier there is an enormous detached tower with many fine walls and grooves along to the right of it, until a section of continuous walls are reached just before a short steep gully containing a small tree is encountered and used for descent. On the right of this descent is an almost separate buttress with various good lines either through the obvious roofs or skirting around them. The tier in worthwhile climbing terms finishes to the right of this buttress with a steep and unfortunately short piece of superb rock covered with just enough of the right sized holds to ensure excellent climbing. To its right is a set of very poor, broken walls with the western descent down a steep terraced slope. There is a large amount of loose rocks and scree at the very top of much of this crag which does make it difficult for belaying and occassionally dangerous for the second who may get showered by the loose debris, knocked off by the rope.

The Climbs

1.   SHADOW   3

    6a + . A hard sustained problem. At the extreme left-hand end of the tier is a black scooped cave or arch with a thin crack 15ft to its right at the only real break in the bulging walls and with a shallow groove above. Climb this faint crack and the groove above with difficulty until established in the upper groove.

Right of Shadow near the top of the walls are two small white-beam trees 60ft apart. The next three routes climb the walls and bulging overhangs between them.

◁ *Inter-Digital Pause, Twilight Tower Buttress*
Climber, Paul Stott

2. **HUNGRY DAYS** 3***

5c + . A strenuous gymnastic route. Starting halfway between the two small whitebeam trees at a thin crack splitting the wall below the left end of the large arching overhang. Climb the thin crack to the overhang and traverse left across the slab to below the small smooth wall and triangular roof. Using undercuts gain the easy scoop and good holds out over the roof to the left and easily up this to the top.

3. **BITTER ENDER** 1*

5b. An appealing line. Start 10ft right of Hungry Days at the white painted square. Climb up to follow the leftward arching roof to its end at a steep crack and the top.

4. **BITTER ENTRY** 2**

5c. A steep technical and committing route. Start as for Bitter Ender at the white painted square. Climb to the arching roof and a crack splitting it at 15ft, follow this through the roof to make a hard move up into the easier angled groove.

Right of Bitter Entry the walls relent and contain three fairly obvious grooves which provide the lines for the next three routes.

5. **TIZER THE SURPRISER** HVS

5a – . Climb the left-hand of the three grooves direct to a good layback crack on the left of a large dubious block halfway up the groove. Gain the top of the block to make an awkward move up to finish.

6. **CENTRAL GROOVE** H Severe

The middle groove directly above a white painted square and arrow. The groove has a smooth left wall in the top half. Pull over the bulge on the right at the top to finish.

7. **THE PANCAKE** Severe

The right-hand of the three grooves with a large dubious pillar on the left at the top.

Right of The Pancake is the obvious enormous detached tower with large chockstones jammed behind it. 10ft left of the base of the tower is a small half buried block with a sharp arête up on its left at a white painted square.

8. **STARTING BLOCK** VS

4b. Start on the block at the white square. Climb up and around the sharp arête into a rock scarred groove on the left which is followed to the top.

9. **RACE RIOT** HVS**
5a. Start as for Starting Block at the white square and climb the open groove directly above. An excellent route on good rock with adequate runners from small wires.

10. **TWILIGHT CHIMNEY** H Severe*
The classic deep chimney up the left side of the tower.

11. **JITTERING TOWER** HVS
5a. On the outside face of the tower is a crack up the left side which cuts through a loose looking overhang at half height. Climb the crack to the overhang, move up left around the arête to a good ledge. Continue up the steep wall to a good runner, traverse right around the arête in a fine position to rejoin the crack in a small groove and up to the top. The crack can be followed direct on a very dubious rock at 5b.

12. **FREJUS** Mild Severe
The chimney up the right-hand side of the tower.

13. **AGAY** Severe
Start as for Frejus but climb the flaked cracks in the wall moving out from the chimney to the right, finish right of a small whitebeam tree.

14. **ANTIBES** Mild VS
4b. 10ft right of Agay is an obvious layback crack starting above a small cave at 8ft, climb this crack.

15. **RUNNING WILD** HVS
5a. Start as for Antibes below the small cave. Move out rightwards with increasing difficulty into a short V-groove. From the top of the groove step left onto the slabby arête and up to finish left of two whitebeam trees.

16. **VOLENTI** Severe*
The deep flake crack trending up to the left and finishing between the two whitebeam trees.

17. **THE GIFT** Severe
Just right of Volenti is a finger crack which is followed to an ash tree at 12ft, move left from this to finish above a small yew tree.

18. **ZILLA** V Diff.
The left-hand of the twin cracks below the large whitebeam tree with exposed roots and the easy ramp up to the left.

19. **FROLIC** Mild VS*
4a. The deep right-hand jam crack to the roots of the large whitebeam tree. Either finish straight up the wall above, or step left and up a short ramp into a small corner left of a small tree.

20. **ROOTS** VS +.

4c. Start behind a large pointed flake just right of Frolic. Climb the black slab to the roots of the large whitebeam tree, step right and climb the steep wall covered with numerous small overhangs.

21. **NO GRIPS** 2**

5b. A surprisingly hard technical climb. Start on top of the large pointed flake. Step onto the arête and climb up rightwards across the slab to a steep finger crack and good runners. Move up and right with difficulty onto the smaller slab and pull over the obvious square cut roof on the left of a sharp prow.

22. **MISSING LINK** Mild VS

4b. 15ft right of the large flake below a square cut roof at 12ft. Climb to the roof, round it to the left and up the steep broken groove to another small triangular roof. Over the roof and up the easier groove to finish left of the sharp arête on dubious rock.

23. **THE LAST FLING** Mild VS

4a. Climb the steep crack with dubious rock on the right of Missing Link to a tiny ash tree finishing on the right of the sharp arête.

24. **CONTINENTAL CHOCS** VS

4b. The steep jam crack filled with chockstones and with a white square painted at its base. Well protected.

25. **PAGODA** HVS*

5a. Strenuous finger climbing to start. On the right of Continental Chocs is a steep broken wall which is climbed direct to the right of three cracks near the top, following the right-hand crack to finish.

26. **RISING CHAMP** Hard V Diff.

A large ash tree grows in a vegetated gully. Climb up the left side of the flake to the ash tree, stepping left to a slab and continuation flake crack above.

27. **MISTY DAWN** Severe*

A good route on excellent rock. Start at the white painted square just right of the large ash tree which is in the vegetated gully. Climb to the deep crack and up the niche above.

28. **SHAKIN STEVENS** VS

4b. On the right of Misty Dawn there is a steep blank wall, bordering the right-hand side of this wall is a broken crack with very dubious rock leading to a large thorn bush. Climb this crack. A dirty 'orrible route.

29. **HAPPY VALLEY**   VS**
4b. A delight worth savouring. Start at a white painted square some 10-15ft right of Shakin Stevens. Climb up trending right into a smooth groove following this to move back left at the top with difficulty and little protection. One can chicken out to the right to finish.

30. **ROCK SPECIAL**   2**
5b. One of the better wall climbs on this crag. Start 8ft right of Happy Valley at the widest part of the undercutting at the base of the wall. Pull over the bulge with difficulty and move up rightwards with few runners across the ever steepening wall to good holds just left of a small bush. Move up and back left onto an easy angled slab and the top.

31. **HOWLING**   1
5a +. Start directly below the obvious groove at the top of the walls and 15ft to the right of Rock Special. Climb the steep wall direct to the groove passing the small bush on its right to the top.

32. **TEN PERCENT SPECIAL,**   2***
5b. On the right of Howling is a pocketed scoop in a slab at 8ft. Gain the scoop (frustrating) and move up rightwards below the overhang into the smooth shallow groove which is climbed to the top. A superb route with not the hint of loose rock.

33. **MASUNGI**   Hard Severe
Climb the flaked blocks direct to the dead yew and live whitebeam trees with a difficult move to gain the trees.

34. **THE AVENGER**   Mild VS
4b. The thin crack line up the wall just right of Masungi gradually gaining in difficulty.

The slabby wall section right of The Avenger has been climbed direct at 5a, but the climbs on this section of rock along to the vegetated descent gully are really getting too short to be worth mentioning in detail. The steep vegetated gully containing a large whitebeam tree is an easy means of descent but if one does not realise this from above it can appear to be a false trail.

50ft right of the descent gully is a 10ft tall flake of rock with a smaller flake on its left. The next route starts on this.

35. **LAND OF THE FAIRIES**   1
5a +. Start on the small flake and climb up leftwards into the

steep hanging groove which gains in enjoyment towards the top.

36. PITMUNGO   Severe
Start between the two flakes at the foot of the cliff and climb either crack to a slab at 15ft with definitely loose large blocks above it. With sense step right and continue more safely to the top.

37. CHATEAU   Mild VS
4a. Just to the right of the larger flake is a white painted square. Climb direct from the square up a broken groove and cracks to the largest whitebeam tree finishing left of it.

38. UNITE   Mild Severe
The obvious deep crack into the niche which is followed to the top.

39. H BLOCK   1
5a. Start at the foot of the crack and smooth groove with a white square a few feet right of Unite. Climb the groove to its top and make a difficult pull over the bulge above onto a slab to move up past a small whitebeam tree to the top.

40. BAY OF PIGS   1**
5b. A fine route with an excellent move across an easy angled slab. Start as for H Block at the white square. Climb up rightwards across the wall to a good crack which is followed to the roof. Move left across the bulging slab and then more easily up cracks.

Right of Bay of Pigs there is an undercut rounded arête with a whitebeam tree in a crack on its right.

41. THE TIGER AWAITS   2***
5b + . A slightly artificial line to start but is worthwhile as the route accepts the challenge of the worst that the buttress has to offer. Start at the foot of the crack containing the whitebeam tree. Traverse out leftwards above the undercut to climb a thin crack in the wall to a dubious hold at 15ft, move up onto this and up the smooth wall above to the arête proper below the large block roof. Step right to a good crack in the roof which is followed to an easy finish left of a small whitebeam tree.

42. THE HEIST   VS*
4c. Start as for The Tiger Awaits. Climb the crack passing the whitebeam tree on its right following the crack up around to the right to an old yew tree. Step left onto the wall, left of the yew, and up to the top.

43. STAY ALERT MALCOLM   HVS*

5a. A fairly long route with some interesting climbing. Start 20ft right of The Heist at a block just left of an ash tree. Move up easily leftwards to a tiny crack on the right of some white marks. Traverse right across the smooth wall to a shallow scoop which is climbed with a difficult move at its top, up to a small roof and good runners. Continue up the broken wall above moving right at first.

Right of Stay Alert Malcolm is a block filled gully and large ash tree which really marks the end of the crag. On its right is a small but superb smooth wall which although it is short does in this case warrant a mention as the climbing is excellent on top quality rock.

44. HYPER MEDIUS MEETS LITTLE FINGER   3***

5c. Exceptional. Start in the centre of the base of the smooth wall at a small white lichen mark. Climb almost direct to a good crack where the angle eases to a slab using pockets, small wire runner on the left.

THE PINFOLD CRAGS (ROCK FARM)

PINFOLD NORTH BUTTRESS
O.S. Ref. 220455   O.S. Sheet No. 117

PINFOLD SOUTH BUTTRESS
O.S. Ref. 222453   O.S. Sheet No. 117

MONKS BUTTRESS
O.S. Ref. 220452   O.S. Sheet No. 117

Situation
The deeply cut Pinfold valley lies up behind Rock Farm some three miles down the Eglwyseg valley from Worlds End heading south. The Pinfold crags consist of three cliffs dominating the rim of this huge amphitheatre type valley, the third of the three small tributary valleys cutting into the escarpment down from Worlds End.

Parking and Approach
Heading south up the hill from Rock Farm MR. 218454 towards Llangollen the lane levels off after 100 yards at a gate on the left, there is a good parking space on the left a little further on.

   The easiest approach to the crags is by the gate following then a good path on the uphill side of a row of full grown thorn trees to a bridge made of railway sleepers, and then up the valley following the left side of the stream to the foot of the Pinfold South Buttress. Although it may appear quicker to ascend the scree slopes directly below the North Buttress and the Monks Buttress, it is certainly not and far more exhausting. The easiest and quickest is as for the South Buttress, via the stream path, and then to follow the base of the tier by good paths to either crags, left to the North Buttress and right to the Monks Buttress.

Access
SEE THE ACCESS NOTES FOR THE EGLWYSEG VALLEY AS A WHOLE

Character and Layout
When approaching the amphitheatre created by the three Pinfold crags, it is immediately apparent that this small valley offers climbing of a quality and character second only to the area's major crag, Craig Arthur.

   Below the watershed at the head of the valley one can view all three cliffs, each offering a high concentration of quality routes on generally excellent rock in fine positions. They range in position and

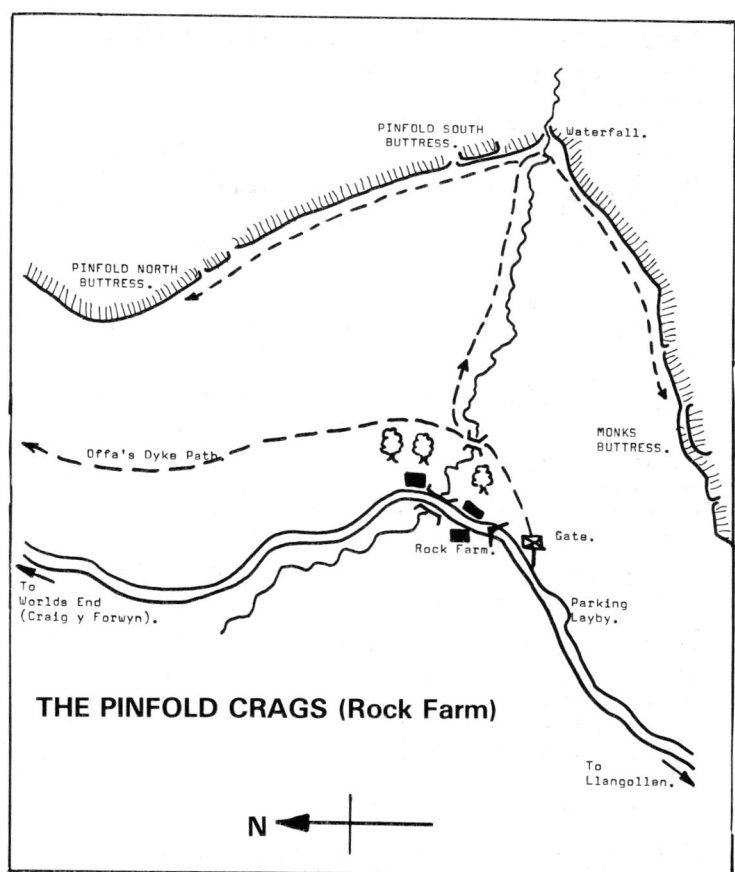

PINFOLD SOUTH
BUTTRESS.

Waterfall.

PINFOLD NORTH
BUTTRESS.

MONKS
BUTTRESS.

Offa's Dyke Path.

Gate.

Rock Farm.

To
Worlds End
(Craig y Forwyn).

Parking
Layby.

THE PINFOLD CRAGS (Rock Farm)

To
Llangollen.

N

character from the steep, highly technical lines climbing the
immaculate undercut walls and grooves of the North Buttress
dominating the left skyline of the valley; through the fine accessible
routes taking the natural lines up scoops, clean-cut corners and
cracks occasionally breaking out onto the blank walls of the South
Buttress which lies just above the watershed; to the spectacular lines
breeching the impressive rock architecture of the Monks Buttress
which broods over the right-hand skyline of the valley.

There are well over 100 routes on this set of crags and there are possibly only a small handful which do not warrant attention. It would therefore be difficult indeed to suggest that one crag is better than another, as each can display an exciting line to tempt any breed of talent.

All the crags dry very quickly as their high position and open aspect often harbours a wind of some description. The Monks Buttress, so named for its silhouette of a monk or hooded figure when viewed from the approach path, appears green and uninviting, yet on close inspection it is found to be quite clean, with an excellent array of routes and certainly it dries as fast as any of the other crags, which is surprising considering it faces north.

PINFOLD NORTH BUTTRESS
O.S. Ref. 220455   O.S. Sheet No. 117. 1:50000

Layout

This extensive buttress stretches for almost 500 yards around the prominent left skyline of the third small tributary valley down from Worlds End.

For almost half the length of the cliff there is an obvious undercut, a feature which is most apparent when viewing the crag from below. This undercut is at its widest in a large bay near the centre of the cliff in turn preventing very little scope for access to the upper walls; three aid routes actually climb the crag in this bay and one free route using a point of aid to start manages to gain the walls.

The cliff is so continuous that there are no breaks throughout its full length for a descent and one has to walk to either end to get down. At the northern end (left facing the rock), there is a huge partially detached flake with two descents down either side and behind it. At the southern end (right facing the rock), one can descend either an obvious grass gully right of the Minor North Buttress, or down the steep broken gully between that buttress and the main cliff, 150 feet left.

All directions are given in relation to when one is facing the rock. At the right-hand end of the cliff (south), there is a separate minor buttress between a steep descent gully on the left and an open grass slide on the right. Start at the right-hand end of this minor buttress just right of a small cave.

The Climbs

1. BLISTER   VS
   4b. Start on a large block just right of a small cave. Make a strenuous lay-back up into a scoop which is followed to the top.

2. SWELL   VS
   4c. Climb the crack above the small cave with a difficult finish to a tree.

3. EXOSTOSIS   HVS*
   5a. Start at a shallow groove 5ft left of Swell below the right-hand end of a spike overhang at 25ft. Climb the groove and thin cracks to the overhang, follow the wider layback crack to the top.

4. CALEFACTION   1
   5b. Climb the layback crack and groove 15ft left of Exostosis to the left end of the overhang. Move up right to pull over the overhang on good holds and back left above to finish up a crack in the wall.

5. FRIGORIFIC   1
   5b. Just right of the dead tree on Auto-De-Fe is a thin crack with a small overhang at two thirds height. Climb to the small overhang move right to another crack and good holds. Poor runners to start.

6. AUTO-DE-FE   Severe
   Climb the grassy holds,the dead tree and the twin cracks above.

7. LAX   Moderate
   The obvious blocked up crack finishing on the left.

8. SCAREMONGER   VS
   4b. Left of Lax is a pillar with a small whitebeam tree top left. Start at the lowest point. Climb up left to the flake crack and the tree to the top.

9. PUGILIST   H Severe
   Climb the chimney on the left of the pillar and with large chock-stones at half height.

10. TRANSIENT   HVS*
    5a. Short but sharp. Start a few feet left of Pugilist and climb the thin crack to a slab on the left at 8ft. Move up the slab and step right onto the wall to avoid the large yew tree and to the top on good holds.

Left of Transient this minor buttress curls round into a steep broken descent gully. On the left of this gully is a large impressive stepped overhang. Between the gully and the large overhang is a slightly vegetated slim groove up the wall with a large flake on its left near to the top.

11. MEGALITH   H Severe
     Climb the slim groove past the small tree.

12. OBELISKS FLY HIGH   H Severe**
     A good route with an exposed finish. Start at the short slab at the foot of the obvious crack on the right of the large stepped overhang. Climb the crack to a large sloping ledge on the right, step left to a ledge on the exposed wall and follow a crack to the top. It is also possible to climb the initial crack direct to finish although this is very loose.

13. WHISPERING WALL   3*
     5e. An artificial looking line but if followed properly it becomes very serious towards the top. Left of the large stepped overhang is a steep wall with a large tree at the top and two small trees growing halfway up. Climb direct to the small trees following a shallow depression and intermittent cracks. Move out right just above the tree into a scoop where it is possible to use a lay-away above. Follow the scoop to the top.

14. TROPHY   H Severe
     The steep groove containing a branchless tree.

15. CENTRE-LINE   VS +
     4c. 8ft right of a large ash tree and holly is a hanging groove at 15ft. Climb direct to the loose looking block at the foot of the groove and on up the groove to the top.

16. ASH TREE RAMBLE   V Diff.
     Climb the broken cracks and groove on the left of the large ash and holly trees.

17. STORM RIDER   3
     5c. 8ft left of the large ash and holly trees are twin cracks in the steep wall. Climb the cracks and tiny corner at the top. A committing route with little protection or good resting places.

The walls become slightly undercut 30ft left of Storm Rider. On the right of a large whitebeam tree at the top of the walls is a distinct yellow right walled corner with a smooth groove on its right, both above the undercut.

18. POISON LETTER   2*
     5c +. Start directly below the smooth groove. Climb the bulge

to a good runner on the left at 12ft (hard). Continue up the groove above with increasing difficulty near the top. A steep fingery route.

19. ORNAMENTAL ART   2*

5c +. Climb as for Poison Letter to a resting place at the foot of the smooth groove. Move down and traverse left, slightly loose, on lay-aways to the obvious yellow hanging corner and up to the top. A fine intricate route.

Left of the hanging corner on Ornamental Art is a slabby cracked wall. Almost in the centre of the wall at its base is a bulge with a broken block pillar on its right leaning against the wall.

20. MAINSTAY   3

6a. Start in the centre of the bulge with a tiny grass filled crack splitting it for a few feet. Climb almost direct to a sharp hand hold at 15ft, move up to easier flaked twin cracks on the left and the top.

21. BASKET CASE   3

6a. Climb as for Mainstay to the sharp hold at 15ft. Move right into a V-groove which is followed to the top.

22. KING OF FOOLS   3**

6a. Start as for Mainstay and up to the sharp hold at 15ft. Traverse out left around a sharp arête and into the yellow hanging corner above the shattered bulge. The best of the three routes sharing the same start.

23. SHASAVAAN   1

5a +. Left of the large shattered bulging overhang is a broken crack leading to the middle of three whitebeam trees at the top, climb this.

Left of Shasavaan are two large yew trees near the top of the cliff, between them are four cracks splitting the wall.

24. WAFER WAY   VS +.*

4c. Climb the right-hand of the twin cracks to the large roof. Climb the roof on good holds. A good route slightly marred by the escapability of the roof moves by using a nearby yew tree.

25. LAST FANDANGO   1**

5b. Climb the left-hand of the twin cracks to an excellent finish up the obvious steep layback crack.

26. HARD FOUGHT   2

5b +. Well protected but strenuous to place. Climb the long straight thin crack left of the orange lichen wall to the left of the square cut overhang, climb this to the top.

27. **CONDESSA** HVS

5a. Climb the overhanging crack to the large yew tree at 20ft. Move left below the tree and climb the deep crack and pillar to the top. Well protected on the difficult start.

28. **SPASTIC SPIDER** 2**

5c. 40ft left of the large yew tree on Condessa are two grooves in the upper half of the cliff. Climb the bulging wall on the left of a thin crack onto a slab at the foot of the smooth left-hand groove. Move up right into the right-hand groove which is followed more easily. A surprisingly good route.

29. **MENTAL TRANSITION** 4****

6a. A truly excellent route with top quality climbing and rock. Start 50ft left of Spastic Spider and just right of a huge block below a steep pocketed groove above the overhang. Climb the overhang using a peg (in place), peg runner above, into the pocketed groove, move up and right to good holds and runners. Continue up the steep slabby wall passing a poor peg runner (hard) into a shallow scoop. Either traverse out left into a square-cut groove which is followed to the top, or climb the shallow scoop direct, the first way is better and the original line.

The walls now end at the right-hand side of a large undercut bay with steep walls and large stepped overhangs. In the centre of the bay the undercut narrows down to a feasible break below enormous stepped overhangs. Two aid routes start here: BULGER.A3 which takes the obvious line up below the stepped overhangs. STEPPING MAN.A3 climbs direct through the bulge from the start of Bulger. Left of Bulger and Stepping Man is the largest single roof on the crag. The roof is split by a crack which runs parallel to the lip of the overhang. DOWNER.A4 follows this crack to a slabby niche above the lip of the roof and then follows a crack out to the right to finish up the steep wall.

30. **ANOTHER REALM** 3

5c. Start as for Downer. An interesting complicated route. Using two nuts for aid under the roof climb to a good hold on the lip and move up into the slabby niche as for Downer, peg runner above. Traverse left along an obvious line for 15ft, poorly protected, to a crack. Continue up leftwards to an ash tree and another tree above and up broken slabs above.

Moving left the walls continue to bulge until a grass rake containing a whitebeam tree, holly, ash and yew is reached. On the left of the rake is a deep rightward trending flake crack.

31. **SMOKEY BEAR** 2
5b. From the foot of the deep flake crack climb straight up then left to a good crack and a dead tree in a broken groove. Strenuous climbing.

32. **MITSUKI GROOVE** HVS*
5a +. 10ft. left of Smokey Bear is a large shallow scoop split by several cracks and large blocks at its base. Climb the cracks from the top of the blocks with a difficult move before stepping right to the top. Sustained.

33. **SPACE ACE** 3**
5c. A technically difficult route. Start as for Mitsuki Groove climbing it for 15ft to traverse left with difficulty to a peg runner at the foot of a slim groove which is followed to the top. It is possible to climb direct to the peg and groove by the pocketed wall, poorly protected, this makes the lead one grade harder all round and very bold.

34. **UNKNOWN FEELINGS** 2***
5c. A sensational route with good protection when most needed. Left of Space Ace is an obvious roof at two thirds the height of the wall. Start directly below its widest part and climb the steep slabby wall to a terrace ledge below it, and a thin flake crack. Climb the roof at its widest with a good hold above the lip, continue more easily up the slabs to the top.

35. **BONE ORCHARD** 3
5c. Technical and committing. Between the start of Kinberg, on the left, and Unknown Feelings, on the right, is a tiny crack petering out at 10ft. Climb the crack and up onto the terrace ledge, move up to a peg runner in a small square-cut corner below the tapering roof. Climb the roof and bulge (hard) to continue up the slab above.

36. **ATLANTIC TRAVELLER** VS***
4c. An interesting traverse in a fine position. Start as for Kinberg and up it for 15ft to the obvious traverse line along the slabby terrace below the overhangs to finish up the cracks at their right-hand end.

37. **KINBERG** VS**
4c. A classic. Climb the fine overhanging corner and crack.

38. **MONUMENTAL** H Severe
Left of Kinberg is an impressive prow of rock above a yew tree. Climb to the yew tree and continue up the groove around to the left of the prow.

Unknown Feelings, Pinfold North Buttress ▷
Climber, Stuart Cathcart

39. **NESTING CRACK** HVS

5a−. The very poor vegetated crack line 25ft left of Monumental, made difficult by the poor quality of the rock.

40. **BOLD POLLY** Severe

Left of the steep arête is a large corner with an overhang at half height.

Left of Bold Polly the walls are severly undercut forming a terraced bay. At the left side of the bay there is a dead tree and wild rose bush at 25ft.

41. **BUFFOON** VS

5a. Climb the short flake crack to the dead tree and wild rose at 25ft. Continue up the broken vegetated cracks and chimney with care.

42. **HIGHWAY HYSTERIA** HVS*

5a. Left of Buffoon is a clump of trees and ivy in the upper half of the cliff. Climb the thin crack and flake wall just left of the trees to the lowest ash tree. Traverse right, below the trees to make a long reach to gain a scoop in the slab on the right. Follow the deep crack. Good climbing.

43. **FREEWAY MADNESS** 3**

5b. A highly recommendable route. Climb as for Highway Hysteria to the lower ash tree. Move above the tree and traverse out left across the steep slab on pockets to a good hold on the yellow lichen. Follow the crack and bulge to the top. The slab can be crossed slightly higher but not as enjoyably.

44. **SENTINAL** 1**

5b. A fine climb with excellent protection. Climb the crack up the wall just right of Bennetto, moving left at the first bulge and then back into the crack following it more easily up and round to the right on a slab. Finish over the bulge at the top of the slab.

45. **BENNETTO** H Severe

Climb the broken corner to the top.

Left of Bennetto the walls bulge forbiddingly again with an undercut base. At the far left end of the undercut a fine crack splits the steep wall just left of a whitebeam tree.

46. **STONED ROMAN** 1

5a+. Climb the thin crack left of the undercut passing a whitebeam tree near the top, move left at the tree to finish up a slab.

47. FRANKO   HVS

5a + . Climb to a crack 15ft left of Stoned Roman and follow it
to an awkward move to gain a grass ledge on the left. Continue
up the deep crack above.

48. FINGERNAIL   1*

5b − . Left of Franko is a steep blank wall with a curving crack
and slab down to the left. Climb the crack and slab to a small
hanging slab below a holly bush. Continue up the steep crack in
the wall on the right moving onto the arête near the top, slightly
loose rock to finish. A far better route than it appears with an
airy finish.

49. SAYFARI   V Diff

Climb the slab and short corner to the holly bush and the block
corner above.

Left of Sayfari is the huge partially detached flake which marks
the northern end of the crag and descent. The right-hand descent can
be ascended as a route at Diff standard the left-hand is not worth
climbing. The face of this huge flake is split by a wide chimney filled
with blocks and can be ascended at about Hard Severe but it is a poor
route. On the left and right of the chimney are two reasonable
routes.

50. SWEET SATISFACTION   H Severe

Climb the groove and layback crack left of the wide chimney.
Enjoyable.

51. FLIGHTING   HVS

5a + . Climb a short wall to a leftward trending layback crack
on the right of the chimney, following this around onto the
right wall of the chimney and the top. Or continue straight up
over the bulge after the short wall. A very loose and worrying
route either way.

The walls on the left (north) of the descent now become short and
broken. There are a few interesting lines which in general have been
climbed but none are really worth going into detail to describe.

PINFOLD SOUTH BUTTRESS
O.S. Ref 222453   O.S. Sheet No. 117 1:50,000

Layout

Following the approach path up the small tributary valley to the escarpment, the Pinfold South Buttress is easily seen on the left at the head of the valley almost beside the stream.

The cliffs very square cut appearance provides numerous top quality corner, crack and fine strenuous wall climbs on good solid rock. On the right-hand side of the cliff are several examples of waterworn scoops which are followed by some of the best routes on the cliff as much of the climbing is on pockets up the very best that limestone can offer. At the left-hand end of the cliff an undercut upper tier comes into play giving five routes which climb the lower main tier, a top pitch which in most cases due to the undercut are not easily won.

The most prominent feature when viewed from below is the deep overhanging crack splitting a massive central block buttress. On its left is a rising line of overhangs which converges nicely with the left wall of the block buttress to stop progress straight up the corner crack, but makes the route which climbs this line continue up the right wall at a surprisingly easy standard.

Descent is possible at either end of the crag, the right-hand end provides the easiest (southern) down the gully which the stream has cut.

The climbs are described from right to left (south to north) when facing the rock, that is **working leftwards from the stream**. All directions are given to mean when one is facing the rock.

The Climbs

1.   MIDNIGHT SPECIAL   2
   5b + . Follow the rightward trending crack 20ft left of the stream and just left of a small whitebeam tree which is near to the top of the crag. A difficult overhung start gains a good resting ledge and the slightly loose, but much easier, crack and short corner to finish.

2.   TOCCATA   VS**
   5a. The good crack on the left of the smooth wall, move left at

the top to avoid loose rock. Well protected.

3. **DEVILS ALTERNATIVE** 1
5b. Climb the smooth groove and scoop with trees near the top. A good route climbing on pockets with protection in the crack on the right.

4. **SOLO IN SOHO** 3***
5c +. An excellent sustained route on perfect rock one of the best on the Pinfold crags. Climb the smooth scoop blocked two thirds of the way up by a small overhang, passing a peg runner. Move left at the overhang to climb the thin layback crack to the top.

5. **RUSSIAN ROULETTE** 1
Climb the slightly loose wall left of Solo in Soho to a small whitebeam tree.

6. **MARANDER** HVS
4c. Up to a sentry box at 10ft by a shattered bulge just left of Russian Roulette. Move left from the sentry box awkwardly up across a smooth slab to a large ledge and the top.

7. **FOOT LOOSE AND FANCY FREE** HVS
5a. The streep strenuous and loose crack left of the rounded arête.

8. **Y CORNER** VS*
5a −. The obvious corner and Y-shaped crack system by either crack, both are about the same grade.

9. **MARNIE** HVS**
4c. Left of Y Corner high up is a short steep hanging groove. Climb direct to the groove and follow it. Just adequate protection.

10. **PHALIC TOWER** 2
5a. Start at a short groove left of the broken rounded arête. Up the groove moving right after 8ft onto the arête and up to the large pending flake. Move left and up to the trees at the top. Poor rock and protection.

11. **NEON KNIGHTS** 2**
5b. An interesting technical route with good protection on small wires. From the small black bay 5ft left of Phalic Tower climb the shallow square cut corner direct using its left edge much of the way.

12. **DEAD OR ALIVE** VS
4b. A dead yew tree and a live whitebeam tree grow at 10ft right of the deep chimney of Eagles Nest Crack. Climb the

corner to the trees, move left below them and up the slabs and walls trending right to the top.

13. **EAGLES NEST CRACK**   H Severe*

The deep chimney crack containing an elderberry bush and a large nest. An awkward finish.

14. **E.C.V.**   VS**

4c. Start by the painted letteres E.C.V. Climb the corner to the overhang and follow the right-hand crack above in a fine position to the large ash tree. An intimidating finsih for its grade.

15. **OVERHANGING CRACK**   1**

5a+. The fine classic crack climbing the very steep block buttress wall. A difficult finish which can only be well protected with very large chocks.

16. **GERALDS DILEMMA**   VS

4c. The square cut corner containing a large block which is avoided by climbing the steep right wall. A worthwhile route.

17. **PROGRESSIONS OF POWER**   3***

The first of the five two pitch routes. A bold technical climb.

Pitch 1.   5c. Start just left of Geralds Dilemma. Climb the steep delicate slab to the overhang and follow this to the arête on the left with a peg runner around to its left. Continue up the crack above to a small tree and a belay on the terrace at the foot of the obvious layback groove. The diagonal line of overhangs rising up from the left to the arête and peg can be easily climbed at the same standard as an alternative start.

Pitch 2.   5c. Climb the main layback groove to the overhang and up the very difficult crack to its left to a poor sloping ledge and the top. An easy escape can be made up to the right around the overhang.

18. **BUSTER BLOODVESSEL**   3**

A serious initial pitch

Pitch 1.   6a. Start at the rightward rising line of overhangs as for the alternative start of Progressions of Power. Climb the bulging overhang and steep wall above for 20ft to a good pocket and runner. Continue to a wizened yew tree and up left to the crawl terrace below upper walls. Move left for 30ft to below a downward pointing flake to belay.

Pitch 2.   5c. Gain the top wall using the downward pointing flake and layback the crack above to a long reach to a small tree and the top.

19. WOOLLY RAMBLE   VS

A poor route which is spoiled by having no real top pitch of its own.

Pitch 1.   4c. Start 6ft right of the deep chimney below a small tree. Climb to the tree, move out right and follow a crack to a smooth wall and continue up to the terrace passing on the right of a large tree. Traverse mainly crawling, right to belay as for Progressions of Power at the foot of the layback groove.

Pitch 2.   4c. Climb the layback groove to the overhang and finish up the cracked wall to its right.

20. PINFOLD RIGHTHAND   Severe*

Left of Woolly Ramble is a huge semi-detached flake the height of the lower walls.

Pitch 1.   Climb the deep chimney and the continuation crack above the chockstone to a belay on the widest part of the terrace.

Pitch 2.   Traverse left for 8ft below a roof and flying rounded arête. stand up awkwardly to climb the roof and easily up the left side of the rounded arête.

21. PINFOLD LEFTHAND   Severe

Start below the deep crack bounding the left side of the huge flake.

Pitch 1.   Climb the fine deep corner and chimney crack with a chockstone which can be passed on the inside by a small man. Belay on widest part of the terrace.

Pitch 2.   As for pitch 2 of Pinfold Righthand.

22. SPLITTING FINGER CRACK   2*

A reasonably good route with a good but poorly protected top pitch.

Pitch 1.   5a. Start below the steep finger crack left of Pinfold Lefthand, and climb this to belay on the widest part of the terrace as for that route.

Pitch 2.   5b. Move left and gain a shallow groove in the upper wall (hard). Follow a slab on the left to the top.

23. LAY ME BACK   H Severe

Left of the thorn bush and below an obvious roof is an obvious layback finger crack. Climb this crack stepping left onto the rounded arête and the top. A fill-in type route.

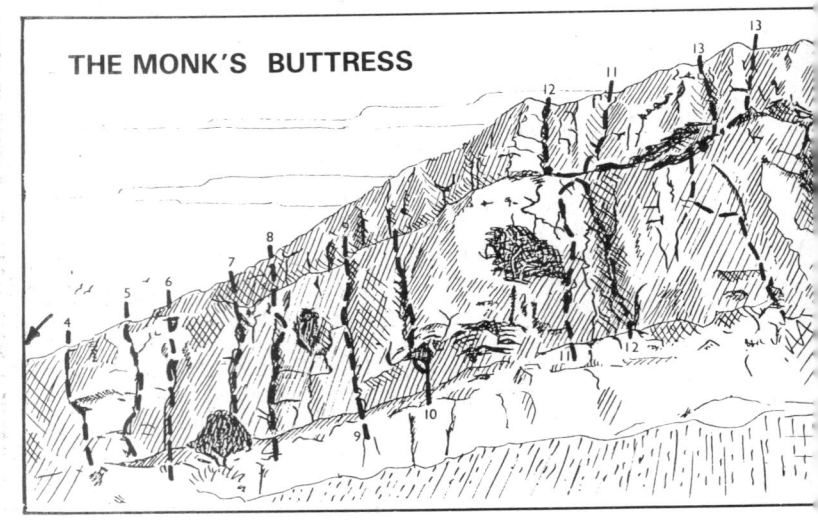

THE MONK'S BUTTRESS

THE MONKS BUTTRESS
O.S. Ref. 220452

O.S. Sheet No. 117 1:50,000

Layout

From the parking layby the crag looms almost straight above. Viewed from this angle the cliff appears to be one large face, but on closer inspection one finds there are three tiers. Only the top tiers are of interest to the climber, and in general they consist of steep walls and overhanging cracks.

The lower of the top two tiers is the largest, with an easy descent down a steep gully left of a fully grown ash tree (east). At the other end of the crag (west), there is another steep gully with a small scree slope at its top also used for descent. To the right of the western descent gully is a separate small buttress with four very worthwhile routes. The Forgotten Buttress.

Almost in the centre of the main tier there is an obvious steep wall, on its left is a large deep zig-zag crack, climbed by a route called Beryl and marks the start of the routes which continue up the top

tier. The steep wall is breeched by a fine steep route, Sir Cuthbert D'Eath, which climbs a faint but compulsive leftward trending bulge. The only other outstanding feature is a strenuous, repelling, overhanging crack right of centre, Jibber, and marks the right-hand end of the two pitch routes.

The routes are described from left to right (east to west) when facing the rock. All directions are given to mean when one is facing the rock. Start at the large almost fully grown ash 50ft right of the left-hand (eastern) descent gully on the tier which is followed from the stream.

The Climbs

1. LUCY   VS +
    4c. Climb the loose broken crack 6ft left of the large ash tree which grows out of a gully and 10ft up.

2. WRIGGLE GULLY   Severe
    Start below the large whitebeam tree some 20ft right of the large ash tree. Move up past the whitebeam on its right and follow the gully to the top.

3. MAINLY FOR PLEASURE   2
    5b. On the right of Wriggle Gully is a black streaked wall. From the middle of the base of this wall climb to a good ledge at

9ft and move up with difficulty rightwards to a point where it is possbible to move back left to a small tree and the top.

4.   THE REBEL   VS**
      4c. The obvious steep left facing corner and flake crack on the left of the small pronounced buttress. A classic route with good protection although difficult to place and very strenuous climbing.

5.   SECOND CHANCE   1
      5b. From a small corner 6ft left of the deep chimney of Grand Laddie, climb the very steep strenuous crack with a difficult mid-section.

6.   GRAND LADDIE   V Diff
      The obvious deep chimney.

7.   AMOCO CADIZ   VS + .
      4c. Climb the groove containing some shattered looking rock 10ft right of Grand Laddie.

8.   ONLY A GESTURE   1**
      5a. 25ft right of Grand Laddie is a clean slabby groove above a short wall. Gain the groove and continue straight up to a bulge. Make a long reach up right to a good hold above the bulge and so to the top. It is possible to finish much easier on the left but this misses out the best part. An enjoyable route.

9.   TOPOLOGY   V Diff
      The green gully crack marking the change from broken walls with a yew tree on the left and steep forbidding walls on the right.

10. FACADE   2*
      5b. Start at the small cave and climb up out of it leftwards on good holds into a steep crack above, continue up the crack on the left. A very testing start.

11. THE HYPE   HVS*
      This is the first of the few routes which make use of the top tier. An interesting route with an exposed top pitch.

Pitch 1.   5a. Start just right of the large ash and yew trees and below a thin crack which leads to a slab at 20ft. Climb the crack with difficulty and the left edge of the slab. Continue up the steep crack in the wall above on good holds to belay on the terrace below the obvious corner on the top pitch of Beryl.

Pitch 2.   5a. Move right along the terrace for 15ft to where the large roof of the undercut starts. Pull over the roof on good holds into a groove which is followed to the top.

12. BERYL VS
Start below the deep zig-zag crack left of the main steep wall.
Pitch 1. 4b. Climb the zig-zag crack to the terrace move left slightly to belay below the steep continuation corner in the upper tier.
Pitch 2. 4c. Climb the continuation corner to the top.

13. SIR CATHCART D'EATH 3***
An excellent sustained first pitch. Start 60ft right of Beryl below an obvious ramp line trending leftwards up the steep wall.
Pitch 1. 6a. Climb the broken crack up leftwards from the slab-through the only real break in the bulging lower wall to a resting foothold and peg runner at 20ft. Move up with difficulty to a flake on the left and a buried peg with a sling above. Climb the ramp stepping left above the peg to good holds and runners. Continue straight up without moving further left. Belay on the terrace in the undercut.
Pitch 2. 5a. Either climb the easy groove behind the belay or more in keeping move right along the terrace and climb the steep crack in the wall behind the large tree growing from the edge of the terrace.

14. THE MANTILLA 3**
A strenuous and technical route. Start at the foot of the crack containing a dead tree at 25ft.
Pitch 1. 5c. Climb the crack to the dead tree and onto the ledge on the left of it. A short square cut corner above is gained and climbed out of up to its right over a bulge with difficulty. Easy ground leads to a tree belay on the terrace.
Pitch 2. 4c. Move left and climb into and up as V-groove type type sentry box to the top.

15. KINSMAN H Severe
Start 20ft right of The Mantilla below twin cracks.
Pitch 1. Climb easily up into the clean corner at 25ft following the cracks above to the terrace, move to the left end of the overhang to a tree belay.
Pitch 2. Gain the broken groove containing the yew tree.

16. THE EVADER VS
Start a few feet left of the big overhanging corner of Jibber, at a crack below the right-hand end of the large block overhang at 25ft.
Pitch 1. 4c. The crack to the block overhang and an old peg runner. Traverse left across the wall below the overhang

following a ramp, descending slightly, to twin cracks. Climb the cracks moving right to the top, belaying on the terrace at the large yew tree.

Pitch 2. 4c. The short overhanging layback crack is undercut to start passing a tree at the top.

17. LIFE   3**
Start as for The Evader. An intimidating and committing first pitch.

Pitch 1. 5c. Climb as for The Evader to the old peg runner and continue up to a good peg runner above the main roof. Move right onto the steep wall, good wire runner level with the peg, and with difficulty gain the yellow groove and up to a small tree and a belay on the terrace.

Pitch 2. 4a. Climb easily up the corner above.

18. JIBBER   1***
A classic strenuous first pitch. Start on the block at the foot of the overhanging corner crack.

Pitch 1. 5b. Climb the very strenuous but well protected overhanging corner crack gaining in difficulty to belay on the terrace.

Pitch 2. 4b. Climb the crack in the wall to a clump of small trees and the top.

19. REALITY EFFECT   3**
A technical bold first pitch. Start on the right of Jibber just right of the steep arête.

Pitch 1. 5c +. Climb straight up on the right of the arête for 15ft move right into the large flake crack which is followed for a short way to where the angle eases. Traverse out left to the arête and move up to a peg runner. With difficulty move up left onto the arête to a good but doubtful hold and the top. Belay as for Jibber on the terrace.

Pitch 2. 4b. Climb to a tree near the top of the upper tier.

20. GINGER CRACK   HVS
5a. Climb the loose crack above the small corner just right of Reality Effect. A difficult move above the bulge is well protected.

21. MALEVOLENCE   VS
4c. Climb the ragged crack to the yew tree which is 25ft right of the arête of Reality Effect. Continue up the wall above.

22. SCATOLOGICAL   Severe
    The vegetated gully to the holly tree and the crack on the right
    to the top.

23. SMOOTH HANDS   Severe
    Start below the whitebeam tree at the foot of the large leftward
    trending overlap. Climb the crack and follow the overlap to the
    top.

24. DESPERADO   5**
    6a. A short but highly technical route with almost no
    protection, a superb test of nerve and skill. Start as for Smooth
    Hands and climb to the tree. Move up on to the slabby wall and
    make a series of very hard moves up into a corner and the top.

25. LITTLE DEAL   H Severe
    On the right of Smooth Hands are three cracks leading to a
    dead tree. Follow the two right-hand cracks to the tree, beware
    of the perched block and follow the groove above.

THE FORGOTTEN BUTTRESS
Right of Little Deal is the western descent gully, right of this is a
small buttress with two obvious undercut grooves on its left face and
a steep wall with a horizontal tree on its right face.

26. CLOVEN HOOF   1
    5b. Climb the left-hand of the two grooves with a strenuous
    start pulling over the bulge into the groove.

27. CODIFY   VS
    4c. The right-hand groove is climbed with an excellent start on
    good holds, finish on the left.

28. GIGOLO   2*
    5b + . Start below the horizontal tree at 10ft which is on the
    right-hand face of the buttress. Climb to the tree and a good
    resting branch. Either continue up the crack above past a
    second tree, or slightly harder but better, move out left halfway
    up th crack above the first tree into a thin crack and up to
    another small tree and the top.

29. THICK AS A BRICK   2
    5b + . An interesting route harder and more awkward than it
    appears. The crack right of Gigolo is climb with difficulty to a
    slab below an overhang. Continue up the crack on the left.

Other routes do exist on the walls to the right (west) of The
Forgotten Buttress, but they are either too short or on very poor rock
and too widely spaced out to be worth describing.

DINBREN CRAGS

1. **ALISON WALLS**
   O.S. Ref. 220446   O.S. Sheet No. 117
2. **ROYAL ARCH WALLS**
   O.S. Ref. 221445   O.S. Sheet No. 117

Situation

As one follows the small approach lane up out of Llangollen into the Eglwyseg valley the first set of crags that are obviously climbable, sitting only a few minutes walk above the Dinbren Farm which lies almost at the junction of the Panorama road and the lane up from Llangollen, are the compact steep walls of the Dinbren Crags. The crag is also the last of the true escarpment crags at the southern end of the Eglwyseg valley and nearest to the main A5 trunk road, set in fourth tributary valley.

Parking and Approach

Except for Worlds End the Dinbren Crags are undoubtedly the easiest cliffs to reach from the valley road. Little advice is actually needed as there is only one real parking place, in a very large passing place/lay-by approximately 100yds south of the T-junction and the Dinbren Farm below the cliffs themselves, MR.219443. The approach is diagonally up the steep hillside skirting above the large thorn trees into the scree filled tributary valley which is followed to the foot of the crags.

Access

SEE THE ACCESS NOTES FOR THE EGLWYSEG VALLEY AS A WHOLE.

Character and Layout

For an easily accessible crag with a high concentration of good to excellent climbs on generally solid rock this section of the escarpment is a must. Although much of the left-hand side, the Alison Walls, are undercut in turn limiting the potential and existence of routes, there are enough very good climbs to make up for this. On the right-hand side this is by no means the case with endlesss lines clamouring to be climbed.

Viewed from just below the cliff it is apparent that there is actually no gap for descent between the two walls — only a very obvious right-angled break up which an easy climb follows. The right-angled

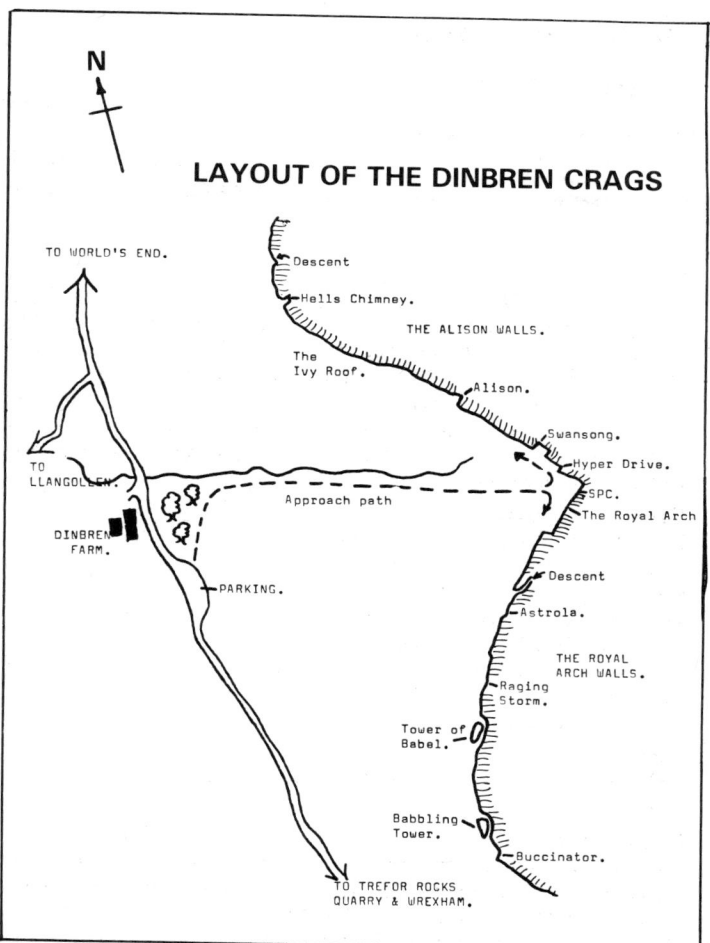

LAYOUT OF THE DINBREN CRAGS

N

TO WORLD'S END.

Descent

Hells Chimney.

THE ALISON WALLS.

The Ivy Roof.

Alison.

Swansong.

Hyper Drive.

TO LLANGOLLEN.

Approach path

SPC.

The Royal Arch

DINBREN FARM.

Descent

PARKING.

Astrola.

THE ROYAL ARCH WALLS.

Raging Storm.

Tower of Babel.

Babbling Tower.

Buccinator.

TO TREFOR ROCKS QUARRY & WREXHAM.

corner does provide a natural break between the walls, to the left (north), the Alison Walls and to the right (south) the Royal Arch Walls.

The Alison Walls are dominated by impressive steep bays, corners, and cracks with the most exciting of these being the crackless corner which Hyper Drive takes a short way left of the right-angled break. Left of Hyper Drive is a bay with a small cave down to its left and continuing on along the undercut walls is the largest corner which is climbed by Gemma's World and Alison. To the left of this large corner is a very tempting yet so far unclimbed smooth wall. Unfortunately the walls become extremely undercut further left with one enormous ivy covered roof. To the left of the ivy roof all that remains is a deep chimney and cave with a descent to the left and a finger ripping overhanging crack with a thread in place to its right. This is the much sought after Punishment of Luxury.

The Royal Arch Walls to the right of the break are so complicated with features that it is almost impossible to describe the layout in detail. Walking right along the foot of the walls the most important features are the large arches, facing left, of the Royal Arches, beyond these is a small pronounced buttress with a deep easy descent gully down behind it to the right. All that remains to be mentioned are the two large towers which dominate the right-hand end of the walls with an uninteresting easy broken wall between. The left-hand tower is the Tower of Babel, which provides a descent down its back and the right-hand is the Babbling Tower. To the immediate left of the Tower of Babel there is a smooth impressive sweep of rock with a short smooth groove which bends over right-wards at the top, Raging Storm, one of the finest routes on this crag climbs this and Hydrogen the wall to its right, both on impeccable rock.

The Alison Walls are described first working from right to left starting at the right-angled corner. The Royal Arch Walls are described from left to right.

The Climbs

ALISON WALLS

1.   SOAP   Hard V Diff
     The obvious deep chimney crack forming a right-angle dividing the two sections of walls at the head of the approach valley. Step left out of the crack at half height to avoid a large chockstone and then back into the crack above to finish.

2.   AMADEAS   HVS –
     4c. Climb the steep crack a few feet left of Soap moving left after 12ft to finish up a good crack.

3.   HYPER DRIVE   3***
     6a + . A very sustained bold route. Left of Amadeus the walls are blank and undercut for 150ft with a steep smooth corner at

the left end. Start on the left of the corner at an old tree stump and just right of a crack which peters out at 15ft. Climb up to above the tree stump and a good runner, traverse right with increasing difficulty into the corner and a good peg runner. Climb the corner past another peg to the overhang and peg runner. Continue straight up the overhanging groove above, hard, or easier move out right from below the overhang onto the arête and up the slab to the top.

4. **YALE** HVS

5a. In the very square cut bay. Climb the right-hand corner with an excellent runner at 20ft.

4A **SWANSONG** 2**

5c +. A fierce route to start. With great difficulty climb the left-hand shattered corner of the bay out over the small cave to start.

5. **SILENT SPIRIT** HVS*

5a. Left of the obvious bay is a large yew tree growing a short way up the broken walls. Climb to the yew tree by a flake crack, passing below the tree to gain a steep slab on the right and up to a sturdy whitebeam tree. An excellent finish after a poor start.

Left of Silent Spirit is a short section of steep blank walls ending on the left with an obvious large open corner.

6. **GEMMAS WORLD** 3

5c. An exposed committing route. Start 6ft left of the foot of the corner. Climb direct to an excellent deep flake at 15ft, traverse right into the corner. Move up a few feet and make a difficult traverse out right across the wall to near the arête and climb the cracks above.

7. **ALISON** 1**

5b. Start as for Gemmas World. Move up and into the corner as for that route but continue straight up the corner to the top.

Left of the last two routes the walls are very undercut and eventually the huge Ivy Roof is reached. 150ft left of the Ivy Roof is a small half dead yew tree.

8. **PUNISHMENT OF LUXURY** 3***

6c. Can there really be a climb more strenuous than this! Climb the pockets in the overhanging wall right of the dead yew tree to a sling in place and a rest. Gain the layback crack and the desperate jam crack above.

9. **HELLS CHIMNEY** Diff.
    Climb the deep chimney up the back of it.

10. **HELLS OWN VARIATION** V Diff.
    Climb the deep chimney as for Hells Chimney moving out left
    at half height to finish on top of the tower.

11. **HELL HOLE** Moderate
    Around and down to the left from Hells Chimney is a small
    hidden hole which is followed upwards inside the tower to its
    top.

12. **HELLO ARÊTE** HVS
    4c. Climb the left outside arête of the Hells Chimney pulling
    out over a loose overhang to start.

THE ROYAL ARCH WALLS

The climbs are described from left to right starting at the right-angled
corner crack of Soap, which forms the natural break between the two
lengths of walls.

1. **SPC** HVS*
    4c. An excellent introduction marred by its shortness. Climb
    the wall up right-wards via hidden holds from the chipped
    letters (SPC) a few feet right of Soap.

2. **SARCOPHAGUS** 2
    5b. 30ft right of the right-angled break of Soap the wall is
    undercut, on the right of this undercutting is a leftward slanting
    crack, start 8ft left of this crack. Move up and left climbing
    above the undercut into a thin crack in the steep wall which is
    followed. Poorly protected.

3. **THE VARLET** HVS*
    5a. The leftward slanting crack.

4. **DEADLY NIGHTSHADE** 2**
    5b. Excellent bold climbing with little protection when needed.
    The blunt arête just below right of The Varlet is climbed by a
    steep thin crack to a bush. Move left around the arête from a
    small bush, hard, to another bush and the top. An easier start
    can be made by coming in from the right across the steep slabby
    wall to the arête.

5. **PEP TALK** VS
    4c. On the right of Deadly Nightshade are steep walls and the
    obvious Royal Arch which curves up and over leftwards. Start
    20ft left of the foot of the Royal Arch below a steep broken

wall. Climb up this wall passing large blocks and up the groove above past a small bush.

6. **THE ROYAL ARCH** 4***
6a. Start at the foot of the obvious overhang line. Follow up the arch line for 25ft where it is possible to move right onto the steep slab, good runner, and up to a deep crack in the slab below the long horizontal roof. Move up to the roof, with good holds above traverse left to where it is possible to pull over into an easy finishing scoop. Exceptional.

7. **A WORLD OF HARMONY** 2***
5b. A fine varied climb. Climb the steep wall below the small ash tree at the right-hand end of the long horizontal overhang. Continue up the corner crack and through the overhang by a good crack to the small ash tree.

8. **DEATH ON MY TONGUE** 2
5c. A serious sustained route. Climb the crack 10ft left of the deep corner crack up the deceptively steep wall.

9. **LET IT RIP** V Diff
Climb the obvious deep corner crack which faces left.

10. **RETURN OF THE GODS** 2
6a. The Fingerlicker of Dinbren. The right wall of the deep corner has a fierce overhanging crack up it which is climbed with good runners.

The Return of the Gods is actually on the face of a huge flake. On the main outside face of the Big Flake is a line of overhangs with two interesting cracks up the right-hand end. Up the back of the Big Flake is a deep easy chimney with a large chockstone jammed at the top, this line is used for a descent.

11. **BIG YOUTH** HVS
5a. Climb the steep jamming crack left of the thin pegging crack on the face of the Big Flake. A slightly harder start can be made on the left.

12. **THANKS TO ELLIS BRIGHAM** 2*
6a +. Climbing at its technical limit most of the way, excellent. The thin crack originally pegged and still containing an old peg.

13. **SUMMER SOLSTICE** 1
5b. On the outside face of the Big Flake left of the whitebeam tree with a good flake crack at 15ft. Climb to the crack which is followed to a good hidden hold high above, move up and right from this. A better route than it may appear.

14. **FIVE O'CLOCK SHADOW** VS
   4c. The obvious corner right of the descent down the back of the Big Flake.

15. **LOOSING GRASP** 2
   5b. Strenuous. Just right of Five o'Clock Shadow is a large Ash tree. Climb the steep crack in the wall on the left of the ash tree, sometimes hidden in summer by the tree itself.

16. **THE PHOENIX** Severe
   Start on the right of the large ash tree down from a large almost dead yew tree. Climb the grass ramp to the yew tree and the broken groove above.

17. **ASTROLA** VS*
   4b. Start down to the right of the almost dead yew tree. Climb easily to a faint crack and slab, move up right to a good ledge and runner. Continue up the steep wall and crack above to finish left of the whitebeam tree. Poorly protected.

18. **THE SCUTTERS** 2
   5b. A worthwhile climb. Start below the deep hand sized pockets in the wall left of a large triangular flake. Climb to the pockets at 8ft and up to the bulge in the wall above, move left to gain a good hold at the foot of the small groove. Pull into the groove and follow it and the corner above to finish right of the whitebeam tree.

19. **EVIL WOMAN** 2***
   5c. A wild route, very strenuous. Start on the right of the large triangular flake at a small corner. Climb the corner crack to a large ledge on the right at 12ft. From the left end of the ledge move up the shattered bulging wall, bold, to a good flake hold at the foot of the obvious steep flake crack. Pull up into the crack and up to the roof, climb up through the roof with a good runner, wire, on the right. Many will ignore this good runner on favour of jibbering as quickly off the route as possible.

20. **FILTH FAZE** VS
   4c. Loose only in appearance. 40ft right of Evil Woman the wall relents with a crack splitting the shattered wall and ends at a whitebeam tree. Climb this crack to the tree.

21. **SALLY IN PINK** VS**
   4b. A classic with good protection. The square cut groove containing two loose looking blocks and an old yew tree.

22. **COLOUR GAMES** HVS**
   5a. Good climbing. Right of Sally in Pink at the top of the cliff

are two large whitebeam trees with a small tree between. Climb the broken cracks and attached flake to the small tree, finish up the superb blank slab from the top of the flake.

23. **RAGING STORM** 3***

5c. Technical wizardry combined with the biggest step in climbing history gains the top. Superb. Start 15ft right of Colour Games at a small rightward facing corner and rib. Climb to the top of the rib to a desperately small wire runner. Move up to the left to the short finger layback crack which arches right at its top and peters out. From a good foothold and small sloping hold at the top of the crack make a huge step right to gain an excellent flake hold, hidden. From this climb directly up the flakes and up the smooth wall above to the top. One can step right at the top of the flake to finish more easily but this ruins the whole character of this great climb.

24. **HYDROGEN** 3***

5b. Bold climbing on perfect rock. Start as for Raging Storm and climb it to the small wire runner. Step right and then up to gain a good foothold by a very balancy move with a good hold above at full stretch. Move up onto this and up to the large block.

25. **THE DEVIL'S ADVOCATE** 3*

5c. A short but sharp interesting climb. On the wall left of the huge Tower of Babel is a smooth steepening groove which is climbed with difficulty and boldness to a small tree.

26. **TOWER OF BABEL** VS

5a. Starting on the outside face of the tower near to the left arête. Climb to a set of easy cracks after a hard start, these lead to the summit.

27. **ANTILLA** Severe

This route climbs the slabby groove and crack between the Tower of Babel and the next huge tower, the Babbling Tower.

28. **BABBLING TOWER** V Diff

Climb the large broken crack which splits the tower front face on its left passing a small tree near the top.

29. **ELECTRA GLIDE** 3**

5c. A serious route with sustained climbing. On the outside face of the Babbling Tower just left of the right arête at a small niche and crack. With difficulty gain the niche and move up to near the old peg on the right. Move up and back left to a good block and into a bottomless groove above the bulge and the top.

30. **DAWN OF DESIRE**   2*
5b. A more interesting and serious route than it appears. Climb the right arête of the tower, at the old peg move up and right onto the inside wall.

31. **SHAKEN NOT STIRRED**   Hard severe
On the wall immediately right of the Babbling Tower is a broken groove which is climbed passing a peg on the right.

32. **CHABRIS**   HVS
5a. On the right of Shaken Not Stirred is a short corner passing on the right of the old peg.

33. **BUCCINATOR**   3**
5c+. An excellent go route. Climb the steep wall right of Chabris by the thin crack mainly on lay-aways on the left to start with good holds on the right near the top by an old peg runner.

34. **GENTLE VIOLENCE**   3
5c. On the slabby wall around the bulging arête to the right of Buccinator. Climb the short crack to a broken slab, move up to the bulge and a good runner. Climb the bulge reaching a good flake on the right and easier ground above passing on the right of a thorn bush at the top.

35. **CASTELLA**   Hard V Diff
The obvious trending crack up to the left.

36. **HAMLET**   Hard Severe
Start as for Castella but climb straight up into the square cut groove, with a difficult move up to gain the foot of the groove passing below a large dubious block.

37. **FIRST GRACES**   Hard Severe*
The excellent layback flake crack above a small ash tree.

The routes finish here at a large fully grown ash tree little else right of this is worth mentioning.

TREFOR ROCKS QUARRY

O.S. Ref. 234433 O.S. Sheet No. 117. 1:50,000

Situation

This very square cut quarry lies 100ft above a layby on the Panorama road around the escarpment above the Dee Valley itself. The top is easily visible from the layby some 300 yards west of the hairpin bends at MR.235432.

Parking and Approach

There is ample parking in the layby directly below the quarry or continuing east to the hairpin bends a rough track leads steeply up to the top rim of the quarry with room for parking at the start of this track. Approach from the main layby is via the steep scree slope or by this track if parked at the hairpin bends.

VEHICLES SHOULD NOT BE TAKEN UP THE TRACK FROM THE HAIRPIN BENDS AS THE LOCAL LANDOWNER USES THIS AREA FOR SHEEP GRAZING.

Character and Layout

Considering that this is only a small quarry, 100ft high, and only a few minutes from the road, the sheerness of its main face can be slightly unnerving on first encounters if one is planning to climb a route on this face.

The holds in general are large and flat with good protection from pegs in place or small wires. The best route yet in the quarry, Any Which Way, takes the full challenge of the main wall at its highest in a superb position and with good protection, it is also a highly photogenic climb.

The south facing walls are more of an easier slab angle, again climbing up horizontal faults and cracks, which provide excellent holds but are poor for protection and so making technically easy routes fairly serious undertakings for the precautious climber.

The Climbs

All directions are given to mean when facing the rock and the routes are described from right to left, that is starting on the slabby wall which is at right angles to the Main Wall.

1.   LINGEN 50ft VS
   4b. Climb the steep slab wall direct starting a few feet right of

119

the extreme right-hand end of the stepped descent in the corner
of the quarry.

2.   WHITE SMEAR   90ft   E4

5c.   A bold and poorly protected route. Start at the corner at
the extreme lower left-hand side of the stepped descent. Climb
the faint crack line in the wall passing a white smear mark and a
large flat hold to make a long reach with no comfort from
runners to an equally difficult finish.

3   THE LAST STRAW   90ft   E2**

5c. Climb the obvious crack 15ft left of White Smear on the
Main Wall with some very difficult moves up to good holds
above half height. A testing route with good protection.

4.   ANY WHICH WAY   110ft   E2***

5b + . An intimidating line connecting the best holds up a steep
wall that is covered with possible holds. Excellent. Start at a
bore hole scar below the widest part of the crawl terrace. Gain
the crawl terrace and pull up onto the steep main wall at a thin
crack which leans slightly right and meets a small overhang at
18ft. Move up, step left and over the small overhang and then
back right to a good rounded quartz flake runner, which is
difficult to see from below, in a horizontal break. Move back
left and up to a large ledge and good resting place and runners.
Traverse right along the footledge for 6ft to a crack which is
followed to the top.

5.   THE SILVER LINE   110ft   HVS

4c. Start on a ledge on the left of the main broken arête at the
left end of the Main Wall. Climb easily up to large blocks and
the crawl terrace. Continue straight up the arête, in a fine
position, to a good crack after a short way, up large holds
above to a large ledge and a small ash tree. Finish wall above
close to the arête on good rock. Belay well back.

6.   GOLD PHLASH   110ft   VS

4b. On the main slabby wall to the left of the Main Wall. Start
25ft left of a whitebeam tree at a sloping grass ledge. Move
easily rightwards to the large dubious blocks on the crawl
terrace. Gain the upper slabs at the obvious small steep left
facing corner, good runner, move leftwards below small
overhangs until it is possible to climb around them and up
direct to the top. Technically easy but a bold route for its grade
due to the lack of protection.

7. **BIG PHLASH** 100ft. VS

4a. Start 20ft left of Gold Phlash and climb easily to the crawl terrace. Climb the short square cut corner with a small overhang at its top, stepping left and up past a good runner to a slim grass ledge. Traverse left along the ledge to finish up the easy groove. Again technically easy but bold for its grade.

BOULDERING

The following list of bouldering places within the area which this guidebook covers, is compiled in order of quality.

CHESTER WALLS   O.S. Sheet 117. MR.402656
HANDBRIDGE OUTCROP   O.S. Sheet 117. MR.406656
Excellent steep fingery wall climbing along the edge of the Roodee Racecourse and around the base of the Grosvenor Bridge which crosses the River Dee alongside the racecourse. The city side of the bridge is the most popular.

The Handbridge outcrop is a short sandstone crag facing the river in the small park visible from the old Handbridge across the river. The climbing is mainly on very widely spaced pockets.

UPPER TWILIGHT GULLY WALLS O.S. Sheet 117. MR.224453
Endless short problems on good rock on the tier directly above the Twilight Gully Walls and the Twilight Tower Crags in the Eglwyseg Valley. Good for an hour after climbing on these crags.

DINBREN OVERHANGS   O.S. Sheet 117. MR.221445
A small compact crag with strenuous overhanging problems, very easy to reach. This is the tier below the right-hand section of the Dinbren crags in the lower Eglwyseg Valley.

WAUN Y LLYN COUNTRY PARK   O.S. Sheet 117. MR.283584
                                     & MR.284580
Two small sandstone quarries only a minutes walk from the parking place at the top of the mountain at Horeb and near to the lake. Perfect quality rock in the nearest quarry to the parking place with some interesting problems.

HOPE MOUNTAIN BOULDERS
(CAERGWRLE)   O.S. Sheet 117. MR.298574
A collection of various sized boulders set in a dip in the hillside just down from the small lane which contours around the east side of Hope Mountain from Cymau MR.294560, at its highest point. Climbing is on an unusual conglomerate rock with few obvious lines.

MINERA OUTCROP   O.S. Sheet 117. MR.268511
An obvious short crag directly above the start of the road which leads over the moors to Worlds End and the Eglwyseg Valley.

Numerous corners and cracks but with a lot of loose rock in places.

CRAIG Y MOCH. (WORLDS END)   O.S. Sheet 117. MR.234482

At the head of the Eglwyseg Valley hidden in the trees to the left of the main Craig y Forwen, (Worlds End). Some interesting steep cracks up short quarried limestone. One excellent overhanging crack and unclimbed wall to its left. A perfect hidden spot for camping away from the tourists.

WHITE QUARRY   O.S. Sheet 116. MR.167759

Broken walls and slabs up to 80ft visible from the Brynford to Pantasaph side wall. Little of worth.

BRYNFORD QUARRY   O.S. Sheet 116. MR180745

A small sunken quarry on the left of the road approaching Brynford from the south-east. Some interesting short problems.

RUTHIN ESCARPMENT   O.S. Sheet 116. MR.122545

A lengthy escarpment with numerous short problems although the rock is occasionally loose or overgrown. Easily seen above the main A494 at Pwllglas three miles south of Ruthin.

CAERGWRLE CASTLE QUARRY   O.S. Sheet 117. MR.307573

Two small short sandstone walls almost within the castle walls at the top of the hill on the south side, the larger wall is smeared with various colours of paint. What there is makes very worthwhile climbing if one is willing to be inventive.

FRITH QUARRY   O.S. Sheet 117. MR.277551
FRITH RAILWAY TOWERS   O.S. Sheet 117. MR.287548

The Frith Quarry is found along the track heading west from Frith up the wooded valley. The quarry is on the right and is very over-grown for getting to but once on the rock, which is a slab of about 30ft, there are a couple of good lines.

The Frith Railway Towers are hidden only a short way up a track heading west from the end of the straight coming south out of Frith. The old towers are on private ground and access is a little uncertain. The climbing is challenging as the towers are up to 90ft high and retreat from the top is difficult. Both towers have been climbed with little protection on the ascents and in both cases the descent was made by two 150ft ropes being tied together with the knot at the top and a rope down either side both climbers abseiled down simultan-eously with friction acting as the main anchor. Other ascentionists are recommended to carry pegs.

GRADED LIST OF CLIMBS IN ORDER OF DIFFICULTY

The following list was compiled from the knowledge of one man's experience of all climbs in this guidebook, it is therefore relatively consistent but hopefully subject to alteration by other climbers at a later date. My main reason for its inclusion is to stimulate others to critically examine it and then improve on it, in turn expanding the wealth of routes in the guide.

The list does not include every route in the guidebook, only a selection of the best routes available.

Very Difficult

Flotta Arête
Inelegance
Let It Rip
Soap
End Flake
Incompetence

Severe

Ganjah
Bush
Plas Uchaf Crack
Volenti
Twilight Chimney
Inspiration
Yobo
White Spring
Half & Half
Obelisks Fly High
Arthur's Pillar
Funeral Corner
Sling
Shattered Crack
Sting
Planerium
Open Book
Misty Dawn
Craznitch Crack
Jennifer Crack

Very Severe

Right Edge
Selva
Ivy Groove
Un-Aided
Astrola
Skullion
Happy Valley
Sally in Pink
Reach
To Cut a Long Story Short
Kinberg
Sunday Driver
Black Out
Wafer Way
The Heist
Attenuation
Epitaph
Picture Arête
Les Elephants
E.C.V.
The Rebel
Ashgrove Prelims
Y-Corner
Toccata
Diamond
Vetta
Durbam Poison
Swlabr

Hard Very Severe

SPC
Single Handed Sailor
Marnie
Coltsfoot Crack
Odysseus
Cima
Silent Spirit
Windy
Exostosis
Race Riot
Highway Hysteria
The Hype
The Corner
Stay Alert Malcolm
Marjoun
Intensity
Vulcer
Pagoda
Charlain
Tripe & Landah
Inter Digital Pause
Fall Out
Knotty Problem
The Arête
Cyclops
Sun Spots
Scrapyard Thing
Yew & Me

E1 or 1 and above

Diagonal Route
The Dog
Overhanging Crack
Hornblower
Gone Bad
Apex
Alison
The Bulger
Tito
The Minstrel
Bay of Pigs
Talking Fingers
Now & Then
Ten Percent Special
Sentinel
Rock Special
Butter Arête
Finer Feelings
Close to the Edge
Jibber
Go-A-Go-Go
Freeway Madness
A Touch of Class
Gigolo
Going Bad
Any Which Way
Tiger Awaits
Spastic Spider
Digitron
Bitter Enemy
High Impedance

Evil Woman
Unkown Feeling
Taerg Wall
Hyper Medius Meets
  Little Finger
Running With The Wolf
Raging Storm
Three Dimensions
Life
The Rasp
The Last Straw
Windhover
Manikins of Horror
Scary Fairy
Heart of Darkness
Swansong
Progressions of Power
Space Ace
Double Crossbones
Buccinator
Whispering Wall
Le Chacal
Craig Arthur Girdle
Bootlace Thread
Hungry Days
Poison Letter

Technical Horrors
E3 or 3 and above

Solo in Soho
Reality Effect
The Fall & Decline
Calculus
King of Fools
Buster Bloodvessel
White Smear
Royal Arch
Mental Transition
Mathematical Workout
Sit Cathcart D'Eath
Gates of the Golden Dawn
Vertical Games
Desperado
Hyper Drive
Swlabr Link
Punishment of Luxury
Shooting Star
Survival of the Fastest

LIST OF FIRST ASCENTS - CRAIG ARTHUR

With the exception of Craig Arthur, most of the crags described in this guide are of outcrop length and do not justify a complete list of first ascents. The most important first ascents are noted in the historical section.

Craig Arthur is a major crag and deserves a detailed list of first ascents.

Climbs	Grade	First Ascent	
Arthur's Pillar	2	Unknown	Pre 1960
Octopus	VS	Unknown	
Scousers	E3/A2	T.Hurley, B.Riley, D.Blythe	1964
Badge	E1	B.Dearman, D.Riley	1965
		1st complete free ascent S.M.Cathcart, T.Curtis	6/4/75

Climbs	Grade	First Ascent	
Scrapyard Thing	HVS	B.Dearman, M.Pedler	1969
	1st free ascent -	S.M.Cathcart	15/9/79
Nemesis	A3	T.Hurley, B.Riley, D.Blythe	1969
Swalbr	VS	B.Dearman, M.Pedler	1969
Craig Arthur Girdle	E2	B.Dearman, D.Riley, T.Herley	1969
	1st complete free ascent	S.M.Cathcart, T.Curtis, M.Cameron	12/5/79
Digitron	E2	S.M.Cathcart, G.N.Swindley	11/6/73
Manikins of Horror	E2	S.M.Cathcart, G.N.Swindley	29/5/76
Stratagem	E2	S.M.Cathcart, G.N.Swindley	28/8/76
Legacy	HVS	S.M.Cathcart, G.N.Swindley	28/8/76
The Deadly Trap	E4	S.M.Cathcart, N.Slaney	22/8/77
The Fall & Decline	E3	S.M.Cathcart, G.N.Swindley	2;/10/77
Cold Finger	HVS	S.M.Cathcart, G.Griffith	20/2/78
Survival of the Fastest	E4	S.M.Cathcart, Unseconded	13/5/78
Tito	E1	S.M.Cathcart, T.Curtis	3/5/80
The Big Plop	E2	S.M.Cathcart, T.Curtis	14/5/80
The Hoax	HVS	T.Curtis, S.M.Cathcart	14/5/80
Gates of the Golden Dawn	E3	S.M.Cathcart, G.Griffiths	15/5/80
Double Crossbones	E3	S.M.Cathcart, T.Curtis	18/5/80
Charlain	HVS	S.M.Cathcart, G.Griffiths	18/5/80
Jungle Warfare	HVS	S.M.Cathcart, P.Stott	21/6/80
Now and Then	E1	S.M.Cathcart, P.Stott	21/6/80
Three Dimensions	E2	S.M.Cathcart, M.Hughes	29/6/80
Scary Fairy	E2	S.M.Cathcart, P.Stott, F.R.Bennett	20/7/80
Monkeys Claws	E2	S.M.Cathcart, J.Dee	8/10/80
A Touch of Class	E2	S.M.Cathcart, P.Stott	13/10/80
Swlabr Link	E3	S.M.Cathcart, N.Slaney	4/6/81
Le Chacal	E2	S.M.Cathcart, D.Whitlow	14/6/81

...enjoy THE SMC Experience

SMC

51-52 WYLE COP
(0743) 241649

Shrewsbury Mountain Centre

127

Printed by Carnmor Print & Design,
95/97 London Road, Preston, Lancashire